BOYS OF THE

The Accidental Role of Church Reforms in Causing and Curbing Abuse by Priests

Vincent J. Miles

Hamilton Books
A member of
The Rowman & Littlefield Publishing Group
Lanham · Boulder · New York · Toronto · Plymouth, UK

Copyright © 2012 by
Hamilton Books
4501 Forbes Boulevard
Suite 200
Lanham, Maryland 20706
Hamilton Books Acquisitions Department (301) 459-3366

10 Thornbury Road
Plymouth PL6 7PP
United Kingdom

Library of Congress Control Number: 2012945060
ISBN: 978-0-7618-5974-1 (paperback : alk. paper)
eISBN: 978-0-7618-5975-8

To Heather, Rebecca, Alex and Georgina,
who make me glad I was never more than a boy of the cloth

CONTENTS

Why did so many Catholic priests molest children?

This is not a question I expected to address when I began work several years ago on a memoir. My original goal was much simpler: to describe the strange semi-monastic existence I led as a teenage Catholic seminarian during the 1960s. While many of our contemporaries were participating in the biggest generational rebellion in history, my classmates and I were quietly and obediently conforming to tradition, praying and studying in splendid isolation. And doing so just a few miles outside Liverpool, whose most famous sons were driving the revolution in popular culture that was a cornerstone of the great rebellion.

But then I discovered that the repressive way of life I intended to describe had a sinister significance: it had been blamed for the abusive behavior of priests towards children that has caused so much pain and scandal in recent years. Which quickly brought me to a modified version of the question posed above. Why exactly did seminaries predispose so many priests to molest children?

For answers to this question I turned to the scientific literature about child abuse—a natural move given that my eventual career was in science rather than the priesthood. And among the many factors that have been theorized to predispose individuals towards sexual abuse, I was quickly able to identify several that were present in the seminary environment I had experienced. The Church-sponsored report that had blamed seminaries for abusive behavior by priests therefore seemed to have been correct.

On other key issues, however, the report was less convincing. The abuse underlying the recent scandals actually occurred decades ago, in an "epidemic" that began in the 1950s and tailed off in the 1980s. Repressive training was not the only factor invoked by the report to explain the behavior of the priests involved, but some of the others seemed inconsistent with the timing of the epidemic; they were developments in society and the Church that occurred too late to have had the influence ascribed to them. The same was true of several factors that supposedly caused the sharp decline in abuse that began around 1980.

The scope of my research therefore expanded once more. If the prevailing explanations of abusive behavior and its decline did not fit with the timing of the epidemic, new insights were needed. To find them I went delving into the history of the seminary system, from its establishment in the sixteenth century to its evolution in the twentieth, and correlated the latter with the recent history of the Church and American society. This led me to two paradoxical conclusions about the abuse epidemic: that it was caused by an ancient reform intended to eradicate rather than encourage clerical corruption; and that it was reversed by modern Church policies that had no obvious connection to sexual abuse.

Then, in May 2011, the Church released another major report on the abuse crisis. In contrast to its predecessor, which was produced to a tight timetable in the aftermath of the 2002 abuse scandal, the new report was based on a carefully executed five-year study. And its conclusions were distinctly different from mine. On close analysis, however, these conclusions did not seem entirely consistent with the data on which they were based. Indeed, they appeared to overlook crucial data that effectively negate one of the report's main arguments, that the abuse epidemic was primarily a by-product of the "permissive society" that developed during the 1960s and 1970s.

Boys of the Cloth therefore stands firm in its unusual conclusions about the abuse crisis. True to its original intention, it still presents an account of the strange way of life in a minor seminary during the 1960s—a period that turns out to be crucial for understanding the abuse epidemic. And true to its expanded intentions, it explains how the ancient reform that established the seminary system led to a modern tragedy, and how the Church fortuitously eliminated some of the most important forces that had created this tragedy.

One issue the book does not address in any detail is the Church's deplorable handling of cases of abuse. All too often, victims received too little sympathy and their abusers too much. All too often, mollycoddled molesters were given new access to young children, with predictable and tragic consequences. And all too often, the Church seemed intent on protecting itself and its priests, but not the young innocents who were being harmed. My decision not to discuss this issue is in no way intended to downplay its importance; like many people, I find the bishops' response almost as appalling as the original abuse. There is little I can add, however, to the excellent critiques of their behavior that others have already produced.

Boys of the Cloth closes by reflecting on the significance of its conclusions for the prevention of abuse by priests in the future. And if just a single child is spared the agony of that experience as a result of the book's existence, every effort that went into its creation will have been rewarded beyond measure.

ACKNOWLEDGMENTS

In the sobering process of writing a book on such an unfortunate subject, the help provided by others has been a rare source of pleasure. This was especially true of the help I received from fellow students at Upholland College whom I had not seen since the 1960s, but was able to track down through the wonders of the internet. Two are near-contemporaries who did become priests, both still in ministry. Monsignor John Devine provided a number of useful leads to sources of information about Upholland, while Fr. John Southworth has been particularly obliging, somehow finding time to provide detailed feedback on the manuscript despite having three parishes to run. Thanks also to Michael Kenna, Mick Power and Professor Jim Bradley for their fact-checking and constructive comments on my narrative about our *alma mater*.

Michael Kenna is now a famous landscape photographer and has published a short book of his own about Upholland, *Boarding School*. Fortunately for me he lets his pictures do most of the talking, leaving plenty of ground for me to cover—and helping me along the way by jogging my memories of the College. Also important in that regard were old copies of the annual *Upholland Magazine* held in the Archdiocesan archive in Liverpool; my thanks to the archivist, Dr. Meg Whittle, for providing access to them. I am also indebted to Rev. Dr. Kevin Kelly, professor of moral theology in the major seminary during my time at Upholland; although we never met while I was there, he generously agreed to critique the book's overall approach and conclusions.

A much less pleasant new acquaintance was the topic of child sexual abuse, particularly as committed by large numbers of priests. After reaching contrarian conclusions about this previously unfamiliar area, I was grateful to my brother-in-law, Dr. Peter Cheetham, for his critical review of the data interpretations in Chapter 8 that are the basis for these conclusions, and to my niece, Dr. Claire Cheetham, for performing statistical analyses on important correlations claimed in that chapter. Dr. David Finkelhor, one of the leading experts on the subject of child sexual abuse, was then kind enough to review key portions of the manuscript and to provide an important suggestion of his own for Chapter 8.

My thanks also to Julia Wilson and Kathy Doherty for their comments on early drafts of the manuscript; to Professor Juliet Schor for good advice and useful introductions; to Fr. Bob Anello of The Catholic University of America, for sharing his knowledge of the seminary system in the US; and to Dr. Karen Terry of the John Jay College of Criminal Justice, principal investigator for two major reports on the US abuse crisis, for her helpful response to an e-mail about the role of minor seminaries in the crisis.

While grateful to all who have helped me along the way, I will close, as authors often do, by claiming sole ownership of any errors in the book that resulted.

CHAPTER 1

THE CALL OF GOD—OR MY MOTHER? "VOCATION," 1961-62

The conversation that changed my life forever took place when I was about ten years old. I told my mother that I wanted to be a priest. This was by no means the first time I had confided in her about my future career plans. Like most young children, I had one new idea after another on the subject. Some ambitions lasted longer than others; I distinctly remember a lengthy racing-driver phase, inspired by my great boyhood hero, Stirling Moss. All of my previous confidences, however, had shared the same fate: they were acknowledged politely and then promptly ignored—interpreted, correctly of course, as the naïve fantasies of a young boy. Had my newfound interest in the priesthood been treated in the same way, it would probably have lasted no longer than the usual few days. But to a devout Catholic woman of my mother's generation, there could be no greater blessing from God than to have a son become a priest. And my mother was much more than devout; she was fanatical. So unlike the host of secular ambitions I had expressed, my clerical ambitions were warmly encouraged. One year later, I was headed off to Upholland College, the seminary for the local Archdiocese of Liverpool.

While the idea of becoming a priest might not even occur to most young boys, in my case it seemed perfectly natural. The Church and its priests were a constant presence in our family. Our Sunday routine included not just Mass in the morning but Benediction in the afternoon. My brothers and I served as altar boys, and attended the parish school with our sisters. My mother typed the handouts for Mass each week. Priests visited our house regularly, and one we knew so well we called him "Uncle." My father's sister and aunt were both nuns. In short, we were extremely Catholic.

Such deep involvement with religion often seems rooted in hardship, and my parents had both experienced their fair share growing up. This was par for the course in the Liverpool neighborhood where they lived, close to the city's docks and associated factories.

My mother grew up in one of the thousands of tightly-packed terraced houses built in the nineteenth century to accommodate low-paid workers in these docks and factories. Even as late as the 1960s, when it was demolished in a slum-clearance program, the house had no electricity or indoor plumbing. I vividly remember visiting my grandmother there. The rooms were lit by gas mantles, and she still cooked on an old-fashioned range built into the fireplace in the back room. The only plumbing was a solitary cold-water tap in a lean-to scullery on the back of the house, and an outhouse in the tiny paved back yard. By the 1950s the upstairs was uninhabitable, and we were always too scared to go up there because we had heard—or imagined—that it had been overrun by rats. If so, the rats were just claiming unoccupied territory, because my grandmother had been living alone for many years. In earlier years she and my grandfather would have needed all the space the house could afford, to raise their family of six children. My mother was the third of these children. Her father was a manual laborer on the Liverpool docks, and his earnings must have barely sufficed for the family's needs. So although my mother was clearly very bright, staying in school beyond the legal minimum leaving age was never really an option. Moreover, just as she reached that age the Great Depression hit, making her earning potential much more important than her education.

Propelled into the workforce, she trained as a shorthand typist and embarked on a career as a secretary. To judge by her accounts of this when we were children, she was fairly successful. She ended up working in the regional office of one of the big film companies, which in those days had significant organizations in the provinces. For good reason: in that pre-television era each company had multiple cinemas in the region, double bills at each one, and a constant flow of new movies to promote. Her boss was quite senior, which resulted in her meeting some of the minor celebrities who came through Liverpool to promote the latest movies. The thrill of these encounters was still obvious to us many years later during her frequent recounting of them.

Although the glamour of the film world may have attracted her, the true beacon in my mother's life was the Church. Our impression growing up was that religion had not been particularly important to her parents; she was the one who embraced the Church with a passion and brought the rest of her family back into it. So strong was her passion that she desperately wanted to become a nun, but the convent turned her down on the grounds of poor health. (Or so we were told as children; we had our own theory about this, which was that the nuns were put off by her intensity.) She threw herself instead into a movement for Catholic workers known as the Young Christian Workers, or YCW, whose mission was to evangelize the workplace. According to its website, the English branch of the YCW was founded in 1937, in nearby Wigan. My mother must have joined soon afterwards and have played a significant role in establishing the organization, because by the mid-1940s she was national president of the women's section. She and my father even spent their honeymoon on YCW business, in 1945, traveling with the national chaplain to Belgium. Since the movement had been founded there in 1925, they must have been attending its twentieth-anniversary celebrations.

A year later, in 1946, my mother gave birth to her first child, my oldest brother. Typically for the era, this effectively meant the end of her work life and of significant activities outside the home. For the rest of her life, another sixty years or so, she was the traditional housewife and mother, bearing and raising children—eight in all—and tending to husband and home. Gone were the movies and the movement, to be replaced by babies and baptisms, toddlers and teenagers, graduations and grandchildren. One thing that never changed, however, was my mother's fierce commitment to the Catholic Church.

§

My father was just as committed to the Church, but much quieter and less intense about it. He too experienced hardship as a child, but for different reasons. In his case, the hardship was brought on by the early death of my grandfather, who died of a perforated ulcer when my father was very young. This was particularly problematical because the family home came with my grandfather's job, as a foreman at a local factory. At the time of his death he had been on the verge of making the major transition into the middle class: he had put down a deposit to buy a house on the Wirral, the peninsula across the River Mersey regarded as "posh" by working-class Liverpudlians. His death brought an end to these plans and to the decent income he had earned, although his employer did pay my grandmother a pension until my father was in his teens.

The family's reduced circumstances caused my father to decline a full scholarship he had been awarded to attend university, a rare distinction in the pre-war era; he was afraid that if he did not immediately start earning, his mother would be forced to work as a skivvy in order to make ends meet. He took a job in what was then a glamorous new industry, aircraft manufacture. When the Second World War broke out shortly afterwards he was spared military service by his childhood bout of rheumatic fever, which was considered to have weakened his heart. He spent the war-time years helping to build Blenheim and Halifax bombers; the Rootes factory where he worked produced over three and a half thousand of these bombers for the war effort.

Like my mother, my father also became very active in the YCW, to the extent that he too was elected national president. He held that position for the men's section at the same time as my mother held it for the women's. This seemed much more surprising in his case, because for his entire life he was very shy and had a slight stammer whenever he was nervous. Growing up, I found it difficult to imagine him going out on the speaking engagements his position must surely have entailed. That he did so, however, was confirmed by a report I once found in an old issue of the College magazine at Upholland (the 1945 issue, I was able to establish from the Archdiocesan archive). This contained a complimentary account of a visit my father had made during the War to speak to the older seminarians about the YCW.

By the time I was born in 1950, my father's YCW days were long behind him. He was now the father of three young children, with every expectation of more to follow. Although forced by circumstances to leave school at a young age, he had continued his education at night school and obtained a technical qualification known as the A.I.M.—Associate of the Institute of Metallurgy. By the early Fifties he was working in an electroplating laboratory for the Automated Telephone & Electric Company (ATE) in Liverpool, which later became part of the Plessey group, and later still of Marconi.

Along the way, he had purchased a small three-bedroom semi-detached house in a Liverpool suburb, borrowing money from my aunt for the deposit so he could take out a mortgage. A few years later we moved to a big old house several miles away, which would have been much more suitable for our growing family—by now there were four children and another on the way—except that my mother took a strong dislike to it. After just a short stay we were on the move again, to another three-bedroom semi about a mile away from the first. This time the move was permanent: my parents stayed there for the rest of their lives, from 1956 until their deaths fifty years later.

If becoming a homeowner had been a major economic step for my father, he took an even bigger one in the early Sixties by becoming part-owner of a business as well. He and several colleagues left ATE to start their own electroplating business in nearby Kirkby, gold-plating electrical components and circuit boards for the emerging computer industry. In one form or another this business continued for more than twenty years, at times quite successfully. Sadly, though, it succumbed in the late Eighties to the general economic malaise that plagued Merseyside in general and Kirkby in particular.

§

The career path chosen by my father tells us something about him that would not otherwise have been obvious to those around him: he was an ambitious man. The clearest illustration of this was his decision to leave the security of ATE and start a new company, at a time when he had a wife and seven young children to support. "Ambitious" is a label he would have resisted, however; his ambition, like his devotion to the Church, was something he kept quietly to himself.

My mother, in contrast, was more overtly ambitious, in much the same way that she was more overtly Catholic. Her drive came from two main sources: a passionate determination to escape the poverty of her youth, and a fierce competitiveness. As a traditional housewife she was limited in what she herself could achieve, and was forced to realize most of her ambitions indirectly, through her husband and children. Since her husband's ambitions were already aligned with her own, she spent much of her energy shaping those of her children, leaving us in no doubt what was expected of us. She and my father had both been denied a higher education by their family circumstances, and now that universities were free for students with strong academic records, she was determined we would be among that group. Academic success on our part would satisfy both of the needs that drove her. On the one hand it would help to ensure financial security for the family. And on the other it would provide excellent material for her favorite new competitive pastime: bragging about her children's accomplishments.

These accomplishments became even more important to her once it became clear that she would lose the one competition she had hoped to win for herself— to become the most prolific breeder in the parish. Her pursuit of this goal was thwarted by a number of miscarriages and at least one stillbirth; to produce her eight children she actually had about twice as many pregnancies. In and of itself this must have been very traumatic for her, but to make matters worse her main rival in the breeding stakes, Mrs. G., forged ahead to produce a total of twelve children. (Or perhaps it was thirteen; I only remember the number went into double figures.)

My mother never quite seemed to get over Mrs. G.'s superior fertility. Her response was to redefine the field of battle, by demanding that her children out-perform Mrs. G.'s in the classroom. In almost every class that had a Miles child there was a G. child as well; heaven help us if we did not finish above our opposite number when the class places (rankings) were announced at the end of each term. But that, we all knew, was the bare minimum required of us. To provide my mother with maximum bragging rights we were also expected to finish top of the class. Often, but by no means always, we were able to meet this expectation. And on the occasions when we failed, first place usually went to one of the G. children, who had the temerity to be bright as well as numerous.

On the economic front, although my father was doing well in his career he had not yet secured the middle-class affluence my mother craved. Whatever his income may have been—a subject he never discussed with his children—he had a mortgage to pay and an ever-growing family to feed and clothe, so money was always tight. My clothes were almost all hand-me-downs from my two older brothers—usually torn or stained, to judge from the rare photographs we have from those days. If any of our shoes developed a hole, my father would improvise a patch with old linoleum cut into the appropriate shape. My mother still treated hot water as the luxury it had been for her growing up: we were allowed one bath a week, the children all sharing the same bathwater, one after another, until it was gray and tepid. And of course, all meals were home-cooked and all journeys by public transportation.

§

One such journey, not long after my fateful conversation with my mother, was to the offices of the Archdiocese of Liverpool. The Archbishop wanted to interview me about my interest in becoming a priest. The interview had been arranged by our parish priest, Father Harvey, the first person my parents had consulted about my potential vocation. Given our involvement in the parish and my regular service as an altar boy, Fr. Harvey knew us reasonably well, and probably had little hesitation in recommending me to the Archbishop. From recent reading I realize that I must have been a good match for the Church's preferred profile at the time: bright, polite, devout and poor (or at least, not too affluent).

The prospect of the interview with Archbishop Heenan was both unnerving and exciting. For the great occasion I was scrubbed perfectly clean, dressed in my best clothes, and doused liberally with Brylcreem to tame my rebellious hair. My mother, who could be almost embarrassingly deferential to mere parish priests, seemed filled with awe at the idea of meeting an Archbishop; as we rode the bus downtown to the Archdiocesan offices, she peppered me with final instructions on how to conduct myself.

The Archbishop turned out to be charming and not at all intimidating. I remember his persona more than our conversation. He exuded a simple dignity, enhanced by his particularly distinguished appearance: graying hair, gold-rimmed glasses, smooth-skinned features, and impeccable episcopal garb. His chief interest, of course, was to find out why I wanted to become a priest. I suspect that my answers to his questions were well-rehearsed platitudes: that I had "this feeling" that God wanted me to devote myself to Him and to helping the sick and the poor. I also suspect that I was able to say this as convincingly as it could be said by any eleven-year-old; I had spent enough time around my mother in the presence of the clergy to know just what tone to adopt.

§

In later years, I came to understand what the genuine answers should have been to Archbishop Heenan's questions. My main reason for wanting to become a priest was simple: the attention and approval it would bring me. Attention from the world in general, and approval from my mother in particular.

In the world I knew, the Church was the most important institution, and the priest was the most prominent and respected person in that institution. Quite simply, I wanted to be the star of the show: the person high up there on the altar, leading the congregation at Mass every week, the one they all revered. My "vocation" was little different from more typical childhood fantasies like wanting to be a sporting hero or a movie star—a product not of conviction but of ambition, inherited in abundance from both of my parents.

If the limelight was what sparked my interest in the priesthood, my mother's reaction was what kept it going. All of a sudden, I had found a surefire way to get her approval, which otherwise was in scarce supply. Only upon deep reflection during the writing of this memoir did I come to realize just how important this was to me. I had never previously recognized how desperate I was at that age for more affection from my mother, and how much this influenced not only my decision to attend Upholland but also my behavior during my first few years there.

Indeed, in multiple earlier drafts of this chapter I grossly understated how important my mother's reaction had been to my pursuit of the priesthood; I only acknowledged my satisfaction with the extra attention she now paid me, and I attributed any previous inattention on her part solely to the demands of raising seven children. In taking this line I was following the habit of a lifetime, that of downplaying the impact of my mother's troubled personality on my own development. This same habit also misled me in my initial drafts of subsequent chapters dealing with my adaptation to life at Upholland, causing me to recount only routine anxieties about being separated from my family, little different from those that might be experienced by any eleven-year-old boy going off to boarding school. Only when I dug deeper into my early memories of Upholland did I remember certain behavior indicating much deeper issues—forcing me to go back and reassess the emotions that drove me there in the first place. And when I did so, I recalled several experiences from my early childhood that suggested or explained an extraordinarily strong need for my mother's attention and approval.

The first of these experiences occurred when I was less than two years old, not long after my sister was born. With Rosemary's arrival my mother now had four children under the age of six, and simply could not cope. She fell into a deep depression and had what in those days was called a "nervous breakdown," requiring her to be confined in a "mental hospital" for several months. In her absence the new baby and my oldest brother were taken in by a neighbor, while my other brother and I were placed in a children's home run by nuns, where we stayed until my mother was released. Although I have few recollections of this experience, it seems safe to assume that by the time I was reunited with my mother I was more than usually anxious for her affection.

Even after my mother was allowed home her mental state was far from stable. During her hospitalization she had been given electric shock treatment, which as practiced in the Fifties was renowned for its brutality; it certainly traumatized my mother. Whether because of this or her underlying personality, she frequently discharged her own brand of high-voltage jolts to her children. With little provocation, usually some minor misbehavior, she would launch into a corrosive tirade against the initial offender, then broaden the verbal offensive to include all of us, berating us for our lack of cooperation, our ungratefulness, our terrible behavior, and our very existence. During these tantrums we would cower together in a huddle, afraid to say a word until the storm broke, which usually involved a dramatic exit by my mother up the stairs to her bedroom, where she would skulk for a while until she had calmed down. These outbursts left us feeling totally unwanted, desperate to find any way to get back into our mother's good graces, willing to do anything to regain her approval.

As a counterpoint, on those rare occasions when her affection flowed as freely as her fury, the effect was soul-warming. One of my happiest childhood memories was the day I found her lost engagement ring. The ring had only been missing for a few minutes, having slipped unnoticed off my mother's finger while she worked in the kitchen, but after a brief unsuccessful search on her own she frantically enlisted my help. In due course I spotted the ring in the murky gap between the cooker and the sink, from where I retrieved it and proudly handed it back to her. She immediately wrapped her arms around me, kissed me on the top of the head, and rewarded me with a sixpence. The hug and kiss were what I valued most: this is the only occasion I can ever remember receiving either from her as a child.

The final episode that came back to me was clearly the progeny of all the others, and one I have never previously mentioned to a living soul. I must have been about eight or nine at the time, and aching for attention from my mother. Aware that she herself always garnered a lot of attention when she was ill, I decided to feign illness, and for maximum impact to do so in a public place. Perhaps with unwitting insight into the root cause of my mother's problems, I chose a location close to our parish church for my charade. After a quick look around to make sure no-one was watching, I lay down on the sidewalk and pretended to be unconscious. My hope was that some Samaritan would come upon me and think I had collapsed, then call an ambulance from the emergency phone box nearby (I had chosen my spot carefully) and have me rushed to hospital. At which point, surely, my mother would shower me with concern and affection.

My plan failed miserably. Nobody came along for several minutes, by which time I was beginning to feel rather silly lying on the ground. I was just about to give up when a middle-aged woman did appear. She helped me to my feet, asked me a few common-sense questions, didn't seem too concerned at my suggestion that I had fainted, and instructed me to walk home slowly and tell my mother what had happened. Which of course I didn't, since by the time I arrived home I was feeling very sheepish, and concerned that my story would attract more trouble than affection.

After this dismal failure, imagine my delight a year or two later when I discovered quite by accident how to secure all of the approval I had been seeking, simply by voicing interest in the priesthood. Ironically, this was not a deliberate ploy for attention but an expression of honest intent on my part. For the reasons explained above, I was genuinely attracted to the idea of becoming a priest. And its attractions became irresistible once I saw my mother's reaction. She was totally enthralled by the idea, which not only appealed to her sentiments as a devout Catholic mother, but also gave her the opportunity for vicarious realization of her own thwarted vocation to the religious life.

From that point forward I became her golden boy, guaranteed to receive more than my fair share of her affection and approval. (To their credit, my siblings never once complained to me about the effect this must have had on them, nor harbored any resentment that I could detect.) Her enthusiasm for my vocation was so great that it would have been impossible for me to change my mind about going to Upholland, even had I been inclined to do so. But the thought never really occurred to me. I had just found the key to staying forever in my mother's good graces, and I was not about to relinquish it.

Compared with the attractions of pursuing the priesthood, the disadvantages seemed negligible. I knew of course that priests cannot marry, but at the age of eleven this seemed unimportant. Eleven-year-old English boys fantasize about scoring goals for their favorite soccer team, not about scoring with the girls; it takes a few more years and waves of testosterone to reverse these priorities. I do remember some of my school friends asking me casually how I felt about the idea of never getting married, but the topic did not command our attention for very long. We preferred to focus on much more pressing questions, such as whether Liverpool FC would finally win promotion to the First Division that year (they did) and which was the best car on the road (no contest: the recently launched E-type Jaguar).

While in theory the adults around me should have made sure that I really understood the commitment I was making, in practice they had no interest in doing so. They would in any case have found the task completely beyond them: sex was the only topic in our household more taboo than money, and none of the priests we consulted could be expected to raise the issue. To be fair, most English adults of that era would have found it equally difficult to tackle the subject with a young boy. But in consequence, I began my pursuit of the priesthood without having even a single conversation with an adult about the toughest sacrifice this would entail.

These insights into my own and my parents' behavior only became clear to me much later, as I was working on this memoir. At the time of my interview with Archbishop Heenan, I was as convinced as my mother that God was calling me to become a priest. I was clearly able to convince the Archbishop of the same, because a few weeks later a letter arrived from the Archdiocese informing us that I had been accepted into the seminary. The stage was set for my new life at Upholland.

§

September 8, 1962, a Saturday: the day I went off to Upholland. The Feast of Our Lady's Birthday, which in my mother's opinion was a most auspicious day for her son to enroll in the seminary—particularly one whose patron saint was St. Joseph, Our Lady's husband. My mother loved such omens.

The weeks before my departure had been a frenzy of preparation, as we worked to gather all the clothing and other items on a list the Archdiocese had sent us. This time, thankfully, there were to be no hand-me-downs; everything was purchased new, apart from the sweaters, which my mother knitted. The seminary seemed suspicious of bright colors, perhaps fearful of their effect on the soul: gray and black predominated, with shirts, sweaters, trousers and socks in the former, blazer and shoes in the latter. When everything was finally assembled we packed it all into a big seaman's trunk, which my father and I had lugged all the way back from a downtown department store on a bus.

With preparations complete and September 8 fast approaching, the big question was how to get to Upholland. The distance door-to-door was about fifteen miles, which nowadays seems like nothing, but in 1962 represented quite a journey. There was no easy way to get there by public transport, especially with a heavy trunk in tow, and we did not own a car. Fortunately, another boy in the parish a year older than me, Brian K., was also entering Upholland, and his parents offered to take me in their car.

And so at last the big day arrived. For me it was almost unbearably exciting: saying my goodbyes to my parents and six siblings, riding in a car for one of the first times in my life, driving through strange places for what felt like hours, and finally reaching Upholland in what seemed the remotest location in the world. As the car turned into the College driveway, Brian and I waited excitedly for the first glimpse of our new home.

By luck or design, the landscapers who laid out the grounds made sure that the College would make a dramatic first impression. From the road, little was visible: a high sandstone wall, sturdy stone pillars flanking the driveway entrance, and a gatehouse just inside. The driveway curved gently to the right for two hundred yards or so, flanked by dense shrubs and tall trees that blocked any sighting of the College buildings. Then, all of a sudden, the driveway broke into the open and there stood the College, so close that it filled the view, monolithic in reddish-brown sandstone.

The first impression was more of a fortress than a school. Two massive wings intersected close to the point where the driveway emerged, joined at the corner by a substantial square tower. Each wing was about a hundred yards long and had three main stories, the lower two generously tall. The wing straight ahead was more elaborate than the other, and was clearly the formal front of the College. The tower at the front corner was matched by two similar structures at the midpoint and far end of the wing, all crested by what looked like battlements; the top floor of each tower even had slit windows, from which the guardians of the faith could presumably fight off the temptations of the world. A two-story portico projected forward from the front of the middle tower, its tall stone arches providing access to the College's formal entrance. Beyond the far end of the wing stood a large chapel, built in the same impressive sandstone, as tall as the three towers, its steep roofline matched and accentuated by an ascending series of smaller gables. The driveway widened into a broad forecourt stretching the length of the main wing; across this forecourt was a large lake, complete with an island, surrounded by attractive landscaping, and connected by a waterfall to a second lake on lower ground.

The formal entrance was not for the use of students, not even—or especially not—on their first day. As we arrived at the corner where the driveway emerged from the shrubbery, we were directed along a fork that went off to the right in front of the other visible wing, at right angles to the main wing. The second wing was less elaborate, with smaller, plainer windows, but just as substantial. Because of the slope of the site, this wing had an extra basement floor along the entire hundred yards of its length. At the far end, another battlemented tower matched those in the main wing—but with one notable addition, an observatory dome on top.

The second wing had no central tower or formal entrance like the other wing, but two arched openings at its midpoint that extended all the way under the building. Through these archways an inner quadrangle could be seen. This was formed by the two wings we had already seen, a third built in the same style and materials, and a fourth that was quite different and evidently older. The open space of the quadrangle was occupied mostly by lawns, terraced on three levels to accommodate the sloping site, with precisely angled banks between levels. The older wing stood on the uppermost of the three levels, dominating the view from the entrance to the quadrangle. A broad path ascended from the archways to double doors in the centre of the older wing, climbing from one terrace to the next via balustraded stone steps.

The older wing was also built in stone, but a pale yellowish stone that had been darkened by accumulated soot. Prominent vertical buttresses at regular intervals divided the façade neatly into equal segments. The center of the façade was dominated by yet another tower, gable-fronted rather than square like the others, its triangular gable projecting above the roofline on either side. In the center of this gable, high above the quadrangle, sat a large and impressive clock, with gold hands and Roman numerals in sharp contrast to its black face. At ground level below the clock was the entrance, two tall doors surmounted by lofty transom windows.

This older wing was the original main wing of the College when it opened in 1883, at which time it housed only the major seminary. Younger seminarians attended St. Edward's College in Liverpool, which had been founded forty years earlier as a school, but had evolved into the minor seminary for the archdiocese. In 1919 the minor seminary moved to Upholland, forcing the major seminarians to be diverted to other institutions for the next few years, until the three sandstone wings and main chapel were completed in 1924. The old main wing then became the base for the youngest three years of the minor seminary, known collectively as the "Lower Line." It was therefore the place to which Brian K. and I were directed on that day in 1962 when we arrived as new seminarians—a right turn at the fork in the driveway, through the archways into the quadrangle, up the flights of stone stairs, to enter through the double doors under the big clock.

Once inside, we were registered and directed to our dormitories. A broad corridor with lofty ceiling and stone floor ran along the rear of the old wing for its entire length. Tall four-paned windows matching those on the façade provided a view to additional buildings at either end of the wing and behind it. At the left end stood the main chapel, at the right end another wing that was clearly also part of the original buildings. As we soon discovered, this other wing was home to one of the most important facilities in the College, the large refectory where we ate all of our meals.

As a first-year, I was in a different dormitory than Brian. His dorm was relatively close and easy to find, on the top floor of the old main wing. Mine was further away, above the gymnasium in a large annex behind the refectory wing. This was a considerable distance from the entrance to the quadrangle, which was the closest point we could reach by car. Somehow or other, though, by means I simply do not recall, the trunk containing all of my belongings was transported from the K. family's car to the dorm.

The dormitory consisted of one very large room with a high, arched ceiling. Its scale can be judged from the function it was given after the seminary closed in the 1980s and became a conference center: it was turned into an indoor archery range. As a dormitory, it was divided by paneled wooden partitions into individual sleeping cubicles, one row around the outside walls and a double row down the middle of the room. Each cubicle provided a small private rectangular space for its occupant, separated by walls or partitions on three sides, with a curtain to close off the front opening at night. A bed, a chair and a small chest of drawers were its only furnishings.

With Brian's parents departed and my belongings unpacked, it was time to begin my new life as a minor seminarian.

CHAPTER 2

SCHOOLS FOR SCANDAL:
THE ROLE OF SEMINARIES IN THE ABUSE CRISIS

Had I been eleven years old in 2002 rather than forty years earlier, I might never have wanted to become a priest. What attracted me, as we have seen, was the prestige of the position; priests really were God-like figures to their parishioners. But by 2002 that prestige was gone, vaporized in a mushroom cloud of sexual scandal. Priests were now more likely to be considered predators than demigods. Nowhere was this more true than in my adopted hometown of Boston, the place where the mushroom cloud erupted.

Boston is like Liverpool in several notable respects: a maritime city with a strong Irish Catholic heritage and an almost religious passion for its professional sports teams, especially the one that plays in red socks. Almost forty percent of the population is Catholic, with large numbers of Italian- as well as Irish-Americans. Bostonians were therefore particularly horrified when one of the most disturbing episodes in the history of the Catholic Church exploded within their own neighborhoods: the clergy sexual abuse scandal.

The revelations that detonated the scandal have been well documented by others, and will be described only briefly here. They began in a newspaper whose role in the saga has often been overlooked, Boston's self-styled alternative weekly, the *Boston Phoenix*. In an article entitled "Cardinal sin" that appeared in March 2001, reporter Kristen Lombardi described shocking allegations by victims of a soon-to-be-infamous pedophile priest, John Geoghan. In civil lawsuits filed in local courts, several victims claimed that Boston's archbishop, Cardinal Bernard Law, had allowed Geoghan to stay in ministry even after he knew that the priest had molested children. When Law admitted as much in a court filing several months later, the story caught the attention of the city's biggest daily newspaper, the *Boston Globe*. The Cardinal and the *Globe* were old adversaries. Back in 1992, angry over media coverage of an abusive priest in a neighboring diocese, Law had singled out the paper for special mention. "The papers like to focus on the faults of the few," he had complained; "...By all means we call down God's power on the media, particularly the *Globe*."

When he invoked the power of the Lord, the Cardinal should perhaps have been more specific about the precise form of divine intervention he was seeking—retribution or inspiration. Nine years later, the paper seemed very much visited by the latter. Inspired by Law's admission in the Geoghan lawsuits, the *Globe*'s Spotlight Team decided to find out how many other priests in the Boston area had molested children, and how much the Archdiocese had known about their activities. And as the team quickly discovered, the answer to both questions was "plenty." But as they also discovered, much of the most telling information was hidden away in records of civil lawsuits that had been sealed by the courts at the Church's request. Undeterred, the *Globe* took the brave decision to challenge the Church in court, petitioning for the release of the records in question, and prevailing on appeal when the court's initial grant of its petition was contested by the Church. After a delay of several months to allow the redaction of personal information about victims, the records were released in batches. And as each new batch appeared, it proved a goldmine for the *Globe* and a minefield for the Archdiocese.

Even before any of the sealed records were available, the Spotlight Team had assembled enough information about John Geoghan to run its first story about him, which confirmed and extended the fundamental details reported by Kristen Lombardi the previous year. Ironically, the story appeared on January 6, 2002, the Feast of the Epiphany—leading to an epiphany of an entirely different sort for local Catholics. Their horror only grew over the next several months, as the *Globe*'s relentless probing and the avalanche of court documents made it abundantly clear that Geoghan's was far from an isolated case. Dozens of Boston-area priests had been accused of abuse; Geoghan may have been the most notorious, but he was simply the worst of many. Almost as scandalous as the number and behavior of the abusers was the way in which local Church authorities had responded. Their prime goal appeared to have been to hide the abuse, with little or no concern shown for the victims. Known predators had been moved away into new parochial assignments, simply providing them with a fresh crop of young parishioners to prey on; victims had routinely been silenced with settlements conditional upon pledges of secrecy.

As outrage mounted over these revelations, Cardinal Law's position became increasingly untenable—even more so after the release of sympathetic letters he had written to several of the abusive priests. In November 2002, a judge ruled that evidence in the Archdiocese's own records contradicted Law's sworn testimony about the reassignment of abusive priests. In early December, fifty-eight Boston-area priests signed a letter asking him to resign. Three days later he traveled to Rome and did precisely that. The significance of this development was aptly summarized by Rev. Richard P. McBrien, a theologian at the University of Notre Dame, in a comment to the *Boston Globe*: "Law's resignation is unprecedented - this is the cardinal-archbishop of one of the premier archdioceses in the whole world - being forced to resign."

§

While Boston remained the epicenter of the abuse scandal, the shock waves quickly spread much further afield. Not long after the first disclosures in Boston, similar stories began to emerge elsewhere. Spurred on by the *Globe*'s example, reporters in other parts of the country began digging into court records in their own jurisdictions, and unearthed similar patterns of individual and institutional behavior: sexual abuse by priests, reassignment of those priests by their bishops, and settlements that silenced victims. The Church and a good part of the nation were in uproar.

In June 2002, in the midst of the uproar, the United States Conference of Catholic Bishops (USCCB) convened in Dallas for its semi-annual meeting. There could be only one topic on the agenda: the abuse crisis. The bishops quickly voted to adopt a document known as the *Charter for the Protection of Children and Young People*, whose key provisions included the establishment of a National Review Board (NRB) charged with investigating the crisis. The Board in turn commissioned the John Jay College of Criminal Justice to conduct a nationwide survey of Church records relating to allegations of abuse in the period between 1950 and 2002. The results of this survey and of the Board's broader investigation were published in separate reports released by the USCCB in February 2004. Both made somber reading.

Taking the John Jay College survey first, this revealed that in the half-century period it covered, 4,392 priests—about 4 percent of the total number in ministry—had been accused of abuse. Over 11,000 children were involved, 81 percent of them boys. The number of complaints rose steadily in the early 1950s, increased significantly for the next two decades, peaked at the end of the 1970s, and then dwindled rapidly during the 1980s. When the results of the survey were first published, some uncertainty remained whether the incidence of abuse had in fact subsided in the 1980s; historically, many victims had taken a long time to come forward, suggesting that additional cases from more recent decades might still emerge and change the picture. This concern has now been laid to rest, however, because most of the complaints filed since 2002 have also involved abuse that occurred decades ago, and fit into the same overall chronology as the cases noted in the original survey. (The report based on that survey will henceforth be referred to as the *Nature and Scope* report, an abbreviation of its actual title, which was *The Nature and Scope of Sexual Abuse of Minors by Catholic Priests and Deacons 1950-2002*.)

In its own report, the National Review Board had no doubt where the blame lay for the "epidemic" of abuse uncovered by the survey: with the seminary system. More specifically, the Board pinpointed two vital functions in which seminaries had failed: in their screening of candidates for the priesthood, and in their preparation of these candidates for the challenges of celibacy.

The failure to screen candidates adequately was largely due, the Board concluded, to a massive surge in their number:

> The significant increase in candidates for the priesthood in the 1950s so overwhelmed seminaries that they did not pay sufficient attention to the strengths and weaknesses of each candidate. One bishop who had served as a seminary rector told the Board that seminaries took in almost anybody who applied during the 1950s, and many of these young men were there not because they wanted to become priests but because of family pressure.

Independently, journalist Laurie Goldstein of the *New York Times* had reached a similar conclusion more than a year before the NRB, reporting in January 2003 that:

> "The priesthood was riding high," said Jay P. Dolan, a professor of history at the University of Notre Dame.... "A lot of boys were entering the seminary..."
> To qualify, a young man needed little more than to say he felt "called" to a priestly vocation. "Getting in the seminary then was a rather easy process," said Mr. Dolan, who entered a seminary in 1954. "There was no screening of candidates at all. They accepted anybody, and the numbers were incredible."

My own experience is completely consistent with these observations. The cursory interview I had with Archbishop Heenan at the age of eleven was the only formal screening I ever underwent in connection with my interest in the priesthood—which was, as we have seen, primarily a gambit to please my mother. And when I arrived at Upholland in 1962 it was full to overflowing: the classes ahead of me had so many students that each was divided into two "streams," and the buildings were about to be expanded for the first time in forty years.

To explain the other key deficiency it had noted about seminaries—their failure to "form" candidates appropriately for the priesthood—the NRB invoked multiple contributing factors. First and foremost was the complete neglect of what the Church now calls "human formation": the development of candidates as well-balanced and mature individuals with a healthy understanding of sexuality and the challenges of celibacy. Far from encouraging discussion of these topics, seminaries had traditionally avoided them, apparently believing that the best preparation for life without sex was to pretend that it did not exist. The sole advice many priests received on the subject of celibacy—often delivered only in Latin—was that they should never be alone with a woman. *Numquam solus cum sola:* "never one man with one woman."

Given the inability of seminaries to deal with sexuality when society at large was still prudish on the subject, it is hardly surprising that they failed to adapt well to the "sexual revolution" of the late 1960s—another factor identified by the NRB as contributing to the inadequate formation of future priests. And at the same time as this radical change in the world outside, seminaries were also coping with fundamental changes within the Church itself. First came the modernizing reforms of the Second Vatican Council, then the open rebellion against *Humanae Vitae*, the 1968 encyclical letter in which Pope Paul VI reaffirmed the Church's ban on all forms of artificial contraception. These developments were, in the NRB's view, a two-edged sword. While they did result in more open discussion of psychological and sexual issues within seminaries, they also created an atmosphere of what the Board called "moral relativism," with seminarians uncertain what code they should live by once the traditional framework that had governed their lives was relaxed; some then behaved as though they were free to do as they wished. In certain seminaries this led to the development of a "gay subculture" during the 1970s and 1980s, a potentially significant factor given that 81 percent of all the abuse victims enumerated in the *Nature and Scope* survey were male.

In essence, therefore, the Board concluded that the failure of seminaries to form men adequately for the priesthood was initially due to their traditional repressive attitude towards sexuality and celibacy, and then to the impact of major upheavals in the Church and society that began in the mid to late 1960s.

By this account, the seven years I spent at Upholland happen to have coincided with a period that is crucial to understanding the role of seminaries in the abuse crisis. When I enrolled there in 1962, Upholland still adhered closely to the traditional form of seminary training now blamed for initiating the crisis, and the Second Vatican Council was just about to begin; by the time I left in 1969, life inside the seminary had changed significantly because of reforms enacted by the Council, while outside its walls, the sexual revolution and the outcry against *Humanae Vitae* were both in full flow. And as the ensuing chapters will argue, the transitions that occurred during this period are indeed crucial to understanding why the abuse epidemic started and ended when it did.

One further observation by the National Review Board adds even greater relevance to this narrative. In its analysis of the deficiencies of the seminary system, the Board was particularly critical of "minor" seminaries—those which, like Upholland, accepted young boys for training. Its concerns about this practice are worth quoting verbatim:

> Numerous individuals interviewed by the Board believe that these boys were denied the opportunity to develop socially and psychologically because of the closed culture of the seminary. Some of these individuals, ordained in their mid-twenties, had the emotional maturity of adolescents. This lack of "normal" psychosexual development may have hindered some of these priests from achieving a healthy celibacy and may explain why some of them sought the company of adolescent boys. The Review Board was struck by the large number of individuals who believed that many offender priests lacked emotional and psychological maturity and considered this phenomenon to be a cause of the incidence of sexual abuse of minors by clergy. The full extent to which such immaturity leads to abuse requires further study.

Time, then, in the spirit of further study, to find out more about the troubling "closed culture" inside these institutions, and its impact on one particular seminarian: me.

CHAPTER 3

A WORLD APART: UPHOLLAND COLLEGE, 1962-63

CHRISTMAS TERM

Rules, rules, rules. Every school has them, Catholic schools famously so. No surprise, then, that rules were high on the agenda that first evening at Upholland, as we gathered in a room known as the "Old Theatre" for a briefing about seminary life. Despite everyone's efforts to look nonchalant and brave, I suspect that most of the other boys felt as I did: nervous about what lay ahead; anxious to make friends (but not wanting to seem so); and itchy in the stiffness of brand-new clothes.

The priest who led the briefing introduced himself as Fr. Shaw, and then addressed us using a strange vocabulary that did nothing to lessen our sense of unease. He was, he informed us, the "Prefect," responsible for discipline throughout the "School" or "Lower House." In this task he would be helped by several men from the "Upper House," or senior seminary, who were referred to as "Minors." Most of us would be going into "Underlow," the first-year class, although there were a few second- and third-year boys who would be joining "Low Figures" and "High Figures" respectively. These three classes were known collectively as the "Lower Line," to distinguish them from the four oldest classes in the School, known

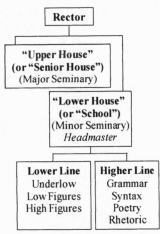

Figure 3.1. Organizational structure at Upholland

as the "Higher Line." And those classes, by the way, were called "Grammar", "Syntax", "Poetry" and "Rhetoric."

Although these names and divisions might all seem confusing, there was only one point about them we needed to grasp immediately: conversation with older seminarians was forbidden. We could talk with other members of the Lower Line, but under no circumstances could we talk with anyone in the "Higher Line" or "Senior House" (as the Upper House was also called). This ban on conversation, we were told, was part of our training in the virtue of obedience.

Speech was not the only activity to be regulated. As Lower Line boys we also had to stay within certain defined areas of the building and the grounds, everywhere else being "out of bounds." Inside, the main area "in bounds" for us was the ground floor of the "old" wing. We were also allowed into a few shared areas like the refectory, the study hall, the gym and the main chapel, but only at certain times for specific purposes. Except for sleeping, our dormitories were out of bounds. Outside, we could use the Quadrangle—but only the paths, not the grass—and the field known as the "Quarry." And on sports afternoons, our games would be on the Lower Line football pitches, beyond the far corner of the Quarry. Those attractive lakes we had seen when we arrived? Completely out of bounds, except for the Upper House and the Professors (as the teachers were known).

One more important rule and our initial briefing would be complete. This one gloried in a fancy Latin name but did not require much translation: *"magnum silentium,"* great silence. From the first ring of the bell for night prayers until the last syllable of grace at breakfast the next day, no talking was allowed. This was another key part of our training in obedience, simple but serious; violations would not be tolerated.

Finally, Fr. Shaw said, we should all get into the habit of writing letters home. Otherwise our families wouldn't know how we were doing, because letters were the only form of communication allowed. And since we wouldn't be going home until Boxing Day, our parents would get very worried if we didn't write.

That's right, Boxing Day, three and a half months away. We had known before arriving that we would be spending Christmas at Upholland, but all of a sudden this seemed impossibly far into the future.

A lot to digest for our first day, as we made our way silently to bed.

§

Since the next day was a Sunday we had the luxury of an extra hour in bed, rising at 7:30 instead of 6:30, which would be our usual time on weekdays. The signal to wake up was impossible to ignore, the loud whirring of a football rattle by the Minor who supervised our dorm. Even so, the Minor made his way around the room checking that everyone was awake, pausing outside each cubicle to conduct a quick exchange in Latin. *"Benedicamus Domino"* ("Let us bless the Lord") he would say, expecting to hear a quick "*Deo gratias*" ("Thanks be to God") in response, and knocking loudly on the partition wall if he did not.

Thanks to our briefing the previous evening, we knew exactly where to go and what to do next—in silence, of course. First stop was the communal washroom in "the Basement" for quick morning ablutions. Since this was a fair distance from the dorm we had to hurry, because we were due in chapel at eight o'clock for morning prayers and Mass.

That very first Mass at Upholland was not particularly unusual, a simple Low Mass in Latin, much like all the other Masses I had attended over the years. This was a little disappointing; I had vaguely expected that Mass in the seminary would somehow be more edifying. Like all the other boys, however, I was on my best behavior, kneeling up straight instead of slumping, reciting the responses crisply, and generally trying to look as devout as I possibly could.

Nor were the surroundings particularly distinguished. The Lower Line had its own chapel on the second floor of the refectory wing, but this was little more than a big rectangular room with an altar, pews and some modest ornamentation. The parish church at St. Margaret Mary's was much more impressive. The main reason for the chapel's existence was the grand scheme within the seminary to keep the different age groups apart. With only occasional exceptions we attended all of our services there, separate from the older seminarians. Indeed, at the same time our Mass was in progress that morning, the Higher Line and Upper House were attending their own Mass in the main chapel.

After Mass we trooped silently back to the dorm to make our beds. Then at last we headed for the refectory, anxious to break both our fast and our silence.

Any disappointment I may have felt over the ordinariness of my first Mass at Upholland did not last long. Later that same morning we had another Mass, a solemn High Mass in the main chapel, which turned out to be the single most uplifting service I had ever attended, in surroundings that were truly spectacular.

This late-morning High Mass on Sunday was the one occasion each week when the whole seminary did gather together, the Lower Line, Higher Line and Upper House all in one place. I had never seen or heard anything quite like it. What made it so special was the music, lilting passages of Gregorian chant mixing with resonant cascades from the huge organ high in the loft above the chancery. The impact was heightened by the restrained splendor of the main chapel: carved oak pews facing each other across the aisle, Gothic paneling on the walls, massive arched windows soaring high above the paneling, and a vaulted oak ceiling supported by elaborate stepped beams. It would have been difficult to attend a Mass like that in a setting like that and not want to be a priest.

§

After dinner (as the midday meal is known in the northwest of England) we had a few hours free before Benediction in the late afternoon, giving us time to get better acquainted with each other and our new surroundings.

Most of my classmates came from other parts of Liverpool, although none that I really knew. A few hailed from less familiar areas of the Archdiocese, towns I could not have placed on a map: Chorley, Leigh, and Ashton-in-Makerfield. Those from outside Liverpool spoke with Lancashire accents, their long vowel sounds and slower delivery a big contrast to the rapid-fire Scouse of the Liverpudlian contingent. Their football allegiances were different, too; they were not all Liverpool or Everton fans, as most of us were. Some even professed more interest in Rugby League than football. The one thing we did all seem to have in common was a large family back home. Nobody had more siblings than me, however; my mother was going to be proud.

While we chatted among ourselves we were also exploring our new environment—being careful, of course, to avoid straying out of bounds. This really didn't leave us much to explore. Inside, we had two areas where we could

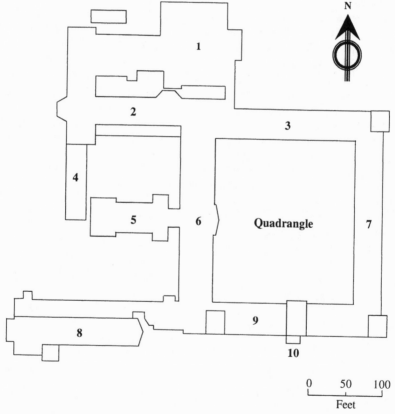

Figure 3.2. Plan of Upholland College. 1: Gymnasium/Underlow dormitory; 2: Refectory/Lower Line chapel; 3: Higher Line wing; 4: New wing (after 1965); 5: Basement (washrooms); 6: Lower Line wing; 7: Upper House wing; 8: Main chapel; 9: Profs' wing; 10: Main entrance.

Aerial view of Upholland College from SSE. Postcard © English Heritage (Aerofilms Collection).

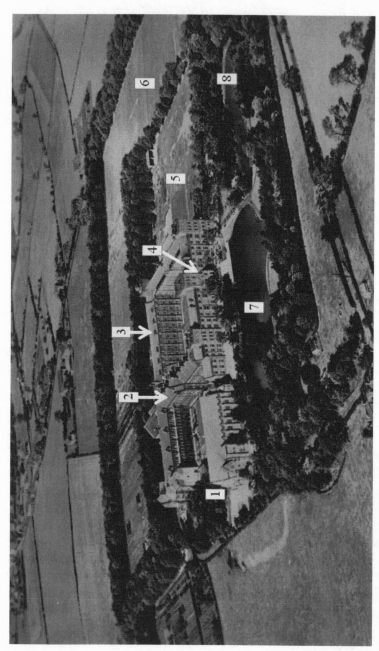

Aerial view of the College from SSW. Key: 1: Main chapel. 2: Lower Line wing. 3: Higher Line wing. 4: Main entrance. 5: The Quarry. 6: Football fields. 7, 8: Upper, lower lakes. Postcard © English Heritage (Aerofilms Collection).

hang out: the Underlow "common room" on the ground floor of the Lower Line wing, and the main corridor of this wing. The common room was little more than a classroom with tables and chairs instead of desks, its main appeal being that it was exclusively ours. The corridor was long and spacious but offered little in the way of recreational opportunities, particularly since the Prefect's office was strategically located right at the midpoint. This location also gave him a commanding view of the Quad, which would presumably limit our freedom to explore some of its more appealing possibilities, like rolling down the grassy banks or racing around the perimeter paths. Beyond the Quad, though, we finally found a place where we would be able to entertain ourselves more freely: the Quarry. Where the name came from I never knew, because the area in question was simply a gently sloping field below the Upper House wing. But it was big, it was open, and it was out of sight of the Prefect's office, making it the best place available for high-spirited fun.

§

The next day we began the regular weekday routine. Wake-up rattle at 6:30, Mass at 7:00, bed-making thereafter, then breakfast—so far just like Sunday, only an hour earlier. Breakfast was followed by half an hour of "spiritual reading," or at least would be on all subsequent weekdays, once we had equipped ourselves with suitably edifying books from the library. Lives of the saints were popular, we were told.

At nine, finally, classes began. By now we'd been up for two and half hours and had spent most of that time on "spiritual" activities, but from this point forward the focus switched to "secular" pursuits. We had lessons all morning, a long lunch break, and then lessons again until tea, which was served at a quarter to five. The only spiritual interlude in this period was a brief interruption before lunch for the Angelus, which we recited in the classroom.

After tea we did go back to chapel again, but only for about fifteen minutes to say a Mystery of the Rosary. We then walked the short distance from our chapel to the huge study hall, where from five-thirty to seven we tackled our "homework" assignments under the watchful eye of a Minor. The study hall was shared with the Higher Line and located on the second floor of their wing, but arranged so that there was no contact between the two Lines. Our entrance and desks were at the front of the room, theirs at the back, and the Minor's desk sat on a raised dais in the open space in between.

The ringing of the bell for supper at seven o'clock signaled the end of the day's work. Having gobbled down our meal in the refectory we finally had some free time, an hour or so, before the bell rang for night prayers at eight-thirty. Silence descended, and our first day as students was over.

§

On Tuesday we had no lessons in the afternoon, but football instead. We would be doing the same again on Thursday afternoon, and make up the time in the classroom by having lessons all day on Saturday. Although this may have been a fair exchange mathematically, somehow it didn't feel that way. The very idea of classes on Saturday seemed unthinkable. Important things happened that day, Football League games in particular; how could we be in the classroom while they were going on? To make matters worse, Saturday evening was going to be just like any other, with the usual hour and a half of study before supper. So much for the weekend!

Our performances on the football field that first week had an impact that went significantly beyond the games themselves. Virtually all of the social and sporting activities in the Lower Line were organized around a "house" system, and the housemasters would be taking turns to pick new recruits based on what they had seen on the football field.

There were three houses altogether, named More, Fisher and Mayne after English martyrs of the Reformation. To me it was immediately clear which one I wanted to belong to: Mayne. This had nothing to do with its patron, who was much the most obscure of the three martyrs—a mere "Blessed" when the other two were "Saints." The key factor was that Mayne played in red, the color of my beloved Liverpool. Fisher might be bearable because they wore green, but heaven forbid that I be picked by More and have to play in Everton blue!

Like many eleven-year old boys I fancied myself a great footballer, the reality being that my enthusiasm greatly exceeded my ability. During the try-out games I ran around a lot and tried to impress, but failed to get more than an occasional touch of the ball, and then to little effect. Luckily, though, I still got my wish. While I may not have been one of the early picks, when the selections were announced I found myself one of the proud new members of Mayne house.

The immediate impact of joining Mayne was social rather than sporting. The inter-house football competition would not start for several more weeks, whereas "house socials" had already begun. These were held in the quarters of our housemaster, Fr. Cheetham. Like all priests on the staff he had a small suite consisting of a bedroom and sitting room; on two or three evenings a week he allowed us to congregate in the latter, during the hour between supper and night prayers.

These "at homes" were usually simple affairs. Most of the time all we did was listen to records and play board games. We could have done almost the same in our own common rooms, but Fr. Cheetham's room was more comfortable and his record-player much better. He was also the custodian of the house's record collection, which contained many more discs than we had in the common room. To keep the collection current we each contributed threepence a week to a "record club," enough in total for Fr. Cheetham to buy two or three new records each week, chosen by popular vote.

The record collection was a big part of my own enjoyment of house socials. At home my parents did not allow us to listen to pop music, and especially not to rock 'n' roll. Ironically, by moving to the seminary I had improved my access to this most decadent form of popular music.

§

Our first Saturday morning turned out to be a rare exception to the routine we would be following on subsequent Saturdays. Instead of classes, the morning was devoted to a special event that was always held on the first Saturday of each new academic year. This event was an uplifting ceremony that underlined Upholland's purpose and provided us a glimpse into our own futures: the ordination of senior seminarians into "holy orders."

Before attending this ceremony I had no firm idea of the steps involved in becoming a priest. Nor did I really understand them afterwards: the lengthy proceedings were conducted entirely in Latin and difficult to follow from Underlow's pews at the back of the main chapel. During my years at Upholland, however, the steps gradually became clear.

The process started with the receipt of the "tonsure," which historically had meant shaving the top of the head so that it looked like a pudding bowl; fortunately for modern clerics, this had evolved into the symbolic removal of just a few tufts of hair. After the tonsure there were four "minor" and two "major" orders before the priesthood itself. In sequence, these six orders were called "porter", "lector", "exorcist", "acolyte", "sub-deacon" and "deacon."

The minor orders were largely symbolic, vestiges of the organizational hierarchy within the early Church. In practice they had been reduced to two composite orders, because the offices of porter and lector and were usually conferred together, as were exorcist and acolyte. Importantly, these orders did not require a vow of celibacy, which meant that seminarians who received them were still free to leave and to marry if they so chose. The commitment to celibacy came with the sub-diaconate, along with a lifetime duty to recite the Divine Office every day. These obligations aside, the sub-diaconate was still largely symbolic, whereas the final order before the priesthood was not: deacons are authorized to preach, to baptize, to conduct marriages, to distribute communion and to officiate at funerals.

At Upholland, senior seminarians were "tonsured" at the start of their third year and ordained as priests at the end of their sixth, having progressed through the various minor and major orders in the interim. To prepare for the September ordinations, the Upper House always started the year with a "retreat"—several days of silent prayer and reflection—beginning halfway through the first week of term.

Because the power to confer holy orders is vested only in bishops or more senior prelates, the ordination ceremony at Upholland usually brought a visit from the Archbishop, although occasionally another bishop would substitute. On my first Saturday at Upholland we were excited to see Archbishop Heenan himself conduct the ceremony. Our excitement was not quite sufficient, however, to last all the way through the lengthy proceedings. In all there were twelve tonsures, two ordinands for exorcist and acolyte, one new sub-deacon, and thirteen new deacons. By the time the last deacon was ordained we were restless; our future might include many long ceremonies in chapels and churches, but our eleven-year-old attention spans were not quite ready for them yet.

§

Teatime that day was the first occasion I was acutely aware of being away from home. Until then I had been sufficiently distracted by the newness of everything around me not to notice. During tea, however, the day's football scores gradually percolated around the refectory, passed on initially to a few boys by one of the housemasters. This was so much a contrast to the exciting Saturday ritual at home that I could not help but feel the difference.

At home, we followed Liverpool's fortunes on a Saturday afternoon almost as religiously as we went to Mass the next morning. In that era we had to rely on the radio for our information; television coverage of sports was primitive, and focused mainly on horse racing, Rugby League and wrestling. Typically, we would tune into the BBC for the half-time scores at a quarter to four, and again an hour later for the final scores and match reports. My father would then prepare the Saturday evening feast that was a family tradition: bacon, black pudding, scrambled egg and fried bread. Having consumed every morsel, I would run to the nearby newsagents for the "Football Echo," a special Saturday edition of the local evening newspaper—printed for some reason on pink paper—with full reports of the Liverpool and Everton games that afternoon. Volunteering for this assignment allowed me to dawdle home and read the Liverpool report before handing the paper over to the family.

This was the routine I missed so much on that first Saturday at Upholland; it was my favorite part of the week at home. Instead of listening avidly to the radio at half-time, I was sitting discontentedly in a classroom. Instead of hearing the scores for myself, I was waiting for word-of-mouth transmission to reach my table. And instead of tucking into the family "fry-up," I was eating bread and jam off a scrubbed wooden table in the junior refectory. The contrast could not have been more stark.

That day's football results were the first news of any sort we had heard since arriving. Contact was limited not only with our families but also with the outside world more generally. No television, radio or newspapers were allowed. As yet we had not been outside the grounds, but when we eventually did so we would be carefully chaperoned. On sports afternoons, for example, we might go out for a walk if the fields were too wet to play football, but a Minor would come along to supervise us. If we were sick we would be tended by Sister Bonaventure, one of the nuns who helped run the household, who would call in a doctor if she felt it necessary. Even for something as mundane as a haircut we would not be allowed outside. Every fortnight, the local barber would be visiting to shear the locks of whichever lucky boys the Prefect felt were in need of a trim.

Clearly, life at Upholland was going to be very isolated.

§

Our isolation may have been unusual, but the subjects we studied in the classroom were not. Somewhat surprisingly, the seminary placed no special emphasis on religious instruction. Seven of the eight subjects on our timetable could have been found at any other school of the period: Latin, French, English, modern history, geography, mathematics, and science. And while the eighth subject was "Scripture & Christian Doctrine," this received no more weight than any other subject, and certainly no more that it would have done at any other Catholic school.

One thing that did distinguish us from other schools was that all of our Professors (as the teachers were known) were priests. For the first few days this definitely felt strange, not because we were unfamiliar with the sight of priests in the classroom—most of us had been grilled on our catechism by them in primary school—but because they were instructing us in secular subjects like history, geography and science. This also seemed a little unfair, making misbehavior in class feel sinful rather than simply disobedient.

Any extra respect we felt compelled to show to our "Profs" in the classroom was less evident outside of it. Like most students we enjoyed gossiping about our teachers' foibles. Fr. Cheetham, for example, the Mayne housemaster and our Latin Prof, quickly became an object of fun because of his shiny bald head. For me this was always hard to understand, since my own father had been bald for as long as I could remember, and so a glistening pate seemed quite normal to me. I had no such difficulty grasping the popular view of the science Prof, Fr. Mercer, who was an object of fear rather than fun. Rumor had it that he had fought in the jungle during the Second World War, where he had learned how to deliver devastating blows behind the ear with a small rubber cosh, now carried in his pocket. None of us were anxious to test the truth of this rumor. Almost as unnerving was Fr. Snape, the mathematics teacher, not because of any purported wartime exploits but by virtue of his height, manner and subject. Our most likeable Prof was the English teacher, Fr. Harvey, who was very earnest but with an undercurrent of friendliness that made him seem more approachable than the others.

Like the other Lower Line classrooms, Underlow's was on the ground floor of the old east wing, overlooking the quadrangle. The room was sparingly equipped, with a blackboard on the front wall, crucifix above it, rows of plain wooden desks, and no decoration or visual aids. Once we entered the room in the morning it became our cell for the rest of the day; instead of moving between classrooms for different subjects—the normal practice in many schools—we stayed in the same room all day, with the Profs doing the walking between lessons. Since the distance they had to cover was very short, there was usually little interruption between one lesson and the next. This made our breaks at mid-morning and lunch even more precious, and the bell for teatime a welcome final escape.

§

Near the end of September we had our first experience of one of the few pleasant surprises Upholland had to offer: an unscheduled "off day." This unexpected treat came at the express request of Archbishop Heenan during his second visit of the month, on this occasion to address the entire seminary about the Second Vatican Council. The Council was about to get under way in Rome, with the Archbishop in attendance, and he wanted to explain its significance to his future priests. After doing so he asked the College Rector, Monsignor Breen, to declare the next day off, a request that was promptly granted.

Off-days like this, we learned, would happen a few times every year, typically to celebrate a visit from some ecclesiastical dignitary or a major news event in the Church, although sometimes just because the weather was fine and the Rector wanted us to enjoy it. We would of course also be off on every holy day of obligation, just as all Catholic schools were.

Being excused from classes did not mean that we were excused from our devotional activities, so the next day we rose at the usual time and attended Mass before breakfast. Instead of lessons, though, we enjoyed impromptu at-homes hosted by the housemasters, longer and more relaxing than the hurried evening socials we had experienced so far. During the Mayne at-home Fr. Cheetham had his radio on, giving us our first opportunity in weeks to hear something about the outside world other than football results. The afternoon was devoted to sports, but by tea-time the fun was over—we had Rosary and study as usual that evening. Our appetite for off-days was whetted, however, and we looked forward enthusiastically to the next one. Patience would be required, though, because unless some other dignitary dropped in unexpectedly, we would have to wait until All Saints' Day on November 1, our first holy day of obligation at Upholland.

§

The week leading up to All Saints' Day passed uneventfully, with little to distinguish it from any other. This might not seem noteworthy, except that the week in question was possibly the most frightening in the entire history of the human race. For several days the world teetered on the brink of nuclear war as the Cuban missile crisis came to a head. At Upholland, however, our isolation was so complete that we had only the vaguest notion that something important was happening.

As the next chapter will explain, the isolation that kept us in such ignorance was an aspect of seminary life that dated back centuries, intended to shield us from "the pleasures of the world." An unintended consequence, as the events of October 1962 showed, was that it also shielded us from the anxieties.

What it also did was create massive gaps in my knowledge of the period in which I grew up. In the case of the Cuban missile crisis, for example, by the time I returned home after Christmas the media had moved on to other stories, so for years afterwards I had only the haziest idea about what had happened. This pattern was repeated time and again with other significant news events.

My awareness of popular culture was similarly affected. This was particularly true for television programs, given that we had no access at all to the medium. When I eventually left Upholland, I was often caught out by conversational references to TV series that my contemporaries had all watched but I had not. I later saw a movie in which the central character was an ex-convict who was trying to keep his past secret, but was given away by his ignorance of events that had occurred while he was incarcerated. I knew exactly how he felt.

§

Two months into my first term at Upholland, I appeared on the surface to have adjusted well to seminary life. Living away from home was not as daunting as it had seemed in prospect, and I spent very little time consciously pining over my separation. The other issues that had bothered me in advance—the typical concerns of new students everywhere, like making friends and adapting to new teachers—were long since behind me.

At a deeper level, however, I was not coping so well, although I can say this only with the benefit of long hindsight. Had I been asked at the time how I was adjusting to my separation from home, I would have said "Fine." Indeed, for many years after I left Upholland, this was effectively what I did say whenever people asked if I had been homesick there. "On the contrary," I always replied, "I was sick of home and glad to get away." While I now see this as a flippant response intended to head off conversation on the subject, until recently I had always felt it to be directionally accurate. I really did not recall many conscious feelings of homesickness, whereas I quickly recognized after I left Upholland that my absence from home had shielded me from many of my mother's more volatile outbursts.

Looking back now, I can see how superficial this assessment was. At the age of eleven I had been cut off abruptly from my family—not just physically separated, which all boarding-school students are, but forbidden almost all contact. Deep down I was reacting in the same way that most eleven-year-olds would: desperately missing the daily interactions with my family, and the sense that someone cared about me. My reaction to this situation had been to go on automatic pilot: each morning I simply jumped out of bed and threw myself into the daily routine, to save me from thinking about how I really felt.

As evidence of my true state of mind, I can recall certain behavior from this period that now seems quite obviously a ploy to draw attention to myself, to establish that I still mattered to other people. This behavior took two main forms. The first was to act goofily and engage in excessively silly wordplays, hoping to earn laughter and approval from my classmates. The second was to visit the Surgery regularly, in search of sympathy from the only maternal figure anywhere in the College, Sister Bonaventure. As she was quick to recognize, most of the time I had nothing wrong with me, other than a need to be mothered.

§

While the isolation of seminary life was undoubtedly the main cause of my subconscious malaise, its rigor must also have played a part. This rigor, I now understand, was the key component of our "spiritual training" for the priesthood. The formal curriculum did not include any instruction in subjects unique to our intended vocation; rather, our spiritual development was expected to flow from the monastic life we led. This was intended to foster good habits of prayer, devotion, sacrifice and obedience—strong foundations for the spiritual life we would lead as priests. Formal training in more directly relevant subjects would take place in the senior seminary.

The routine at Upholland certainly provided us with ample opportunity to develop appropriate habits of prayer and devotion. In a typical week we attended eight Masses, engaged in spiritual reading for three hours, said the Angelus six times, recited seven Mysteries of the Rosary, attended seven sessions of night prayers, and went to confession once. Higher Line boys did even more, rising earlier to meditate for half an hour before Mass every day, adding another three and a half hours of prayer to the week.

Similarly, sacrifice was an integral part of our daily lives. This was most obvious in the isolation we endured from our families, but there were many other examples too. The absence of television, radio and newspapers. Our confinement to the grounds. The general austerity of our existence—typified by lumpy beds in basic cubicles, mediocre food eaten from scrubbed wooden tables, and sparsely furnished common rooms.

As for obedience, this was an ever-present requirement from the moment we woke under one night's *magnum silentium* to the moment we fell asleep under the next's. During the waking hours in between, we were required to show obedience in a host of different ways: by rising as soon as the rattle sounded, arriving in chapel on time, showing unquestioning respect for the Profs all day, refraining from conversation with the older boys, staying "in bounds" at all times, studying in silence for ninety minutes every evening… and so on.

Violations of the rules were taken seriously. Minor infringements were usually penalized with a detention and "lines," sitting in a classroom repeatedly writing some apposite statement such as "I must pay attention in French class." While this type of sanction is probably still common in schools today, the penalty meted out for more serious infractions has long since fallen out of favor: corporal punishment. At Upholland this was administered using a thick leather strap known as the "Tan." The Prefect decided how many "strokes" were appropriate for the misdeed in question, then administered these across the hands. From my one experience of the Tan, I can testify how painful it was and how effective this made it as a deterrent. Decades later I can still recall the pain, but not the offence for which I was being punished.

§

For eleven-year-old boys, time has a peculiar elasticity. When I first arrived at Upholland, Christmas and the end of term had seemed impossibly distant; now, suddenly, December was upon us, with so much to do before Christmas there barely seemed time to fit it all in.

By tradition, the highlight of Christmas Day was an evening pantomime staged by Underlow, and featuring every boy in the class. This year's performance was to be *Dick Whittington & His Cat*, based loosely on the folk tale but actually a satire on events at the College during the year. (Or so we learned when the review appeared in the *Upholland Magazine* months later; this fact was completely lost on us at the time.) The whole show was put together by several of the staff over a period of three weeks leading up to Christmas. Since we also had end-of-term examinations to take, those weeks were particularly busy.

For me there was an extra event in the middle of the month, my birthday. At home this would have been a special day, more for the attention I received than for anything else, given that our presents were usually modest and we never threw birthday parties. At Upholland, however, the day passed almost unnoticed. My friends did of course wish me a happy birthday, and a card arrived from home, but that was it. No cake, no presents, no fuss. Even though I had reached the grand old age of twelve and wanted people to think of me as grown up, I couldn't help feeling somewhat sorry for myself.

Also putting a damper on my birthday were the examinations that started right after it. As I was well aware these would bring significant expectations, not so much from the Profs but from my mother. The results would be used to determine "class places," and I knew which place she would expect of me. As I began my revision I was not particularly optimistic about winning that place: I had slipped badly down the ranks during my last year at St. Margaret Mary's, and after three months at Upholland was known more for my silly behavior than anything else. But I was determined to do my best.

The exams were held during the last week of term, and by Christmas Eve the results were ready. To learn how we had done, we had to suffer through an elaborate public ordeal known as "*Locorum*" (Latin for "of places"). This was held in the gym, which also doubled as the school auditorium—we would be performing our pantomime there the next day. The entire School was present, Higher Line as well as Lower Line, with all of the teachers seated on the stage. One class at a time, the boys in each class filed out into an open space in front of the stage, and stood in a line across the room waiting for their places to be announced. As each boy's numerical place and name were read out, he would bow to the Profs on the stage and make his way back to his seat. Adding extra anxiety to the occasion, the entire proceedings were conducted in Latin.

When Underlow's turn came we all trooped out and lined up, listening intently as the stream of Latin began, not yet familiar enough with the language to catch every word, and afraid of not recognizing our own names when they were announced. In my case I did not have to wait very long. No sooner had the reader begun than he announced "Primus, Vincentis Miles." Given my reputation as the slightly goofy class clown, these words must have surprised most of the people in the room that day. None was more surprised than me. At first I thought I had misheard, and hesitated before making my bow. Then, confused but gratified, I returned to my seat.

I mention this experience not to brag—who would care about my place in a small class almost fifty years ago?—but because of its impact on two important constituencies. The first was my mother, the second my classmates.

For my mother, my first place would be a perfect Christmas present, an academic triumph she could brag about to her friends, and especially to Mrs. G. With deep satisfaction I imagined what her reaction would be; I was now guaranteed an even warmer welcome on Boxing Day than my long absence had already ensured.

When it came to my classmates, the impact of my surprising first place was less uniformly positive. On the one hand I was now established, at least temporarily, as the class "swot." While not nearly as desirable as being the best footballer or tallest boy, this status did give me some sort of credibility, and meant that I would not have to work quite so hard for attention. On the other hand my classmates now had less reason to tolerate my sometimes silly verbal antics—and in due course, as we shall see, their reduced tolerance had significant consequences for me.

§

Christmas Eve was a busy day, our next assignment being the dress rehearsal for the pantomime. Most of us were in the chorus, me included, with just a line or two each in the script. When we first saw our costumes we were quite taken aback: flouncy white shirts, baggy satin pantaloons, short black waistcoats and little fez hats. These outfits were re-used every year for the chorus, and must have been purchased originally for a pantomime with an Arabian theme—Ali Baba, perhaps? Fortunately there were nineteen of us with identical costumes, which helped us to feel less self-conscious about wearing them.

That evening we did not have our usual night prayers at eight-thirty, but stayed up late so we could attend Midnight Mass in the main chapel. Fires were lit in the Lower Line common rooms—the only time in the year when this was done—and several of the Profs came round and told stories by the fireside. While we would all much sooner have been in our own homes, we were definitely enjoying the build-up to Christmas, and increasingly excited that our return to those homes was now so close.

Midnight Mass itself was a joyous affair. Our whole life at Upholland was geared to following Christ, and Christmas Day was treated as the most important birthday in the history of the human race. We celebrated accordingly, especially during the singing of our favorite Christmas carols during Mass. Creeping silently to bed that night, I was totally exhilarated.

On Christmas morning we rose late, had breakfast and then attended a jubilant High Mass. The festive air continued for the rest of the day, with a big Christmas dinner followed by a film in the afternoon, and then our pantomime in front of the whole College that evening. The audience laughed a lot—perhaps from amusement at the script, perhaps because of our many miscues, or perhaps out of sheer joy at the prospect of going home in the morning.

§

Boxing Day at last. For once we were glad to jump out of bed as soon as the rattle sounded, and happy that Mass was so early. After wolfing down breakfast we were free to leave. In my case this meant teaming up again with Brian K. and looking for his parents, who had agreed to give me a lift home. One hundred and nine days had passed since they first delivered us to Upholland, one hundred and nine days during which I had neither seen nor spoken with my family. It was indeed time to go home.

My reception there was all I could have wished. Everyone gathered around me excitedly, commenting on how I'd grown, firing off questions about Upholland, and generally shining with enthusiasm at seeing me again. My parents were of course delighted with my school report and my first place in class. And they were determined to make Boxing Day every bit as much a family celebration as the day before had been. To cap it all, snow was falling heavily outside, the perfect accompaniment to my deferred family Christmas.

The snow that fell on Boxing Day ushered in one of the coldest winters on record in the United Kingdom, with the weather dominating my two-week break at home. The temperature rarely rose above freezing and we had frequent further snowfalls. Like many houses of the period ours had no central heating, so we spent much of our time clustered around the fire in the living or the sitting room, only darting away when absolutely necessary.

As my mother quickly made clear, daily Mass fell into the "absolutely necessary" category for me. No matter what the weather outside, she expected me to find my way to the parish church; I might be on holiday from the seminary, but as far as she was concerned there was no such thing as a holiday from my religious obligations. So every morning I put on my warmest clothes and dutifully headed out into the bitter cold, starving hungry because I had skipped breakfast so I could take Communion. Although the church was barely half a mile away, it seemed much further with fresh snow on the ground and a blustery wind in my face. By the time I got home again after Mass I'd had quite enough outdoor activity for the day. Even a walk to the local park would have been treacherous and toe-numbing; the warmth of the living room fire seemed so much more attractive.

EASTER TERM

After two shivery but enjoyable weeks at home it was time to head back to Upholland. The bitterly cold weather continued, ruthlessly exposing the limitations of the College's central heating system. "Central" this may have been, but "heating" seemed beyond its capabilities. The sadness of leaving home again was compounded by the discomfort of being cold most of the time.

Four of my classmates did not return. One term of our isolated monastic life had been enough for them. In my case, the question of leaving so quickly never really crossed my mind. As far as I was concerned I had made my decision to become a priest, and that was the end of it. Even had I considered leaving, the thought of telling my mother would have quickly deterred me. I knew how much she was counting on me to fulfill her dream, and would have been terrified by the consequences of disappointing her. Which is possibly why the thought never arose in the first place.

The frigid weather did at least bring some compensation in the form of new recreational activities. By the time we returned in early January the Upper and Lower Lakes were frozen solid. The wind had blown much of the snow off the surface of each lake, and over the next few days a group of the senior seminarians cleared the rest. We then had two magnificent areas for skating, each larger than a typical suburban ice rink, providing wide open spaces for experienced skaters and novices alike. My classmates and I were all in the latter category, but after hitting the ice almost daily for the next seven weeks, were well on our way to the former.

The other new activity made possible by the arctic conditions was sledding. The farm attached to the College had several steeply sloping fields ideal for this purpose, all blanketed in deep snow, and the miscellaneous sports gear available from the Prefect included several decent toboggans. All but one of these had wooden runners, which provided a reasonably quick descent that seemed quite exciting—until, that is, we had the chance to experience the same descent on the lone sled with metal runners. Decades later, I still vividly remember my first ride on this rocket, plummeting downhill with my face just inches above the packed snow, then bailing out into the deep snowdrift at the bottom of the hill. Sheer exhilaration!

§

By the time the snows retreated and the ice melted, Lent was almost upon us. With the distractions provided by our winter sports the term had flown by until this point; now, however, the penitential tone and additional hardships of Lent quickly dampened the mood, and the calendar slowed to a crawl.

Although my own mood was also affected by Lent, for the most part I went about my daily business with the same unthinking cheerfulness as before, never consciously aware that below the surface I was feeling increasingly deprived of attention. Occasionally, however, my behavior would provide a more accurate indication of my subconscious mood—most notably in an incident that occurred on the football field not long after normal sports afternoons were resumed.

On the day in question I was playing in goal, a position I really liked because of the opportunities it provided for diving around in the mud. An energetic dive was in fact a key factor in the incident, as I threw myself sideways to save a fierce close-range shot from one of the opposing forwards. The ball beat me completely but then cannoned back off the foot of the post— smack into my temple as I landed on the ground just a few inches away. The force of the impact certainly stunned me, and may actually have caused me to lose consciousness for a few moments. The next thing I knew I was looking up at the sky with a whole group of boys gathered solicitously around me. My attendants also included Fr. Cheetham, who decided that I needed to be carried off the field. By that point I had probably recovered enough that I could have stood up, shrugged off my painful encounter with the ball, and gotten on with the game. Instead, I milked the incident for all it was worth, allowing myself to be carried not just off the field but all the way back to the Lower Line wing, a considerable distance. Being the centre of all that attention and concern was just too irresistible.

Not long after this incident we began our annual retreat, a major opportunity for self-reflection. Whatever great insights this gave me about myself, they did not include recognition of my attention-seeking behavior for what it was.

§

The retreat was part of a marathon of prayer and services that occupied all of Holy Week. The week started gently enough with Palm Sunday, which we observed with our normal Sunday Masses and schedule. In the evening, however, we began three and a half days of prayer, spiritual reading and introspection, all conducted under a strict rule of silence. The only words we were allowed to speak were our responses during services; no conversation of any sort was permitted. For young boys living in close quarters, three days without speaking to one another was an almost impossible challenge. We all took it very seriously, though, glaring conspicuously and self-righteously at any classmate who lapsed into speech, however briefly.

The week's intensity continued even after the retreat ended on Thursday morning and we could finally talk again. The next three days were Maundy Thursday, Good Friday and Holy Saturday, the most solemn days in the Christian calendar. In addition to the long traditional services on Thursday evening and Friday afternoon that commemorate the Last Supper and the Crucifixion, we had further lengthy sessions in chapel for "Tenebrae"—a morning service named after the Latin word for shadows, and part of the Divine Office for the last three days of Holy Week. The Divine Office is a standard set of prayers that priests must recite every day of their lives, an obligation that many monks fulfill by singing the prayers in Gregorian chant. We adopted the same practice for Tenebrae, whose mournful chants set a funereal tone for the rest of the day. Indeed, on Good Friday evening and all of Holy Saturday the College went into mourning for Christ's death. Even outside of chapel we were expected to conduct ourselves accordingly, conversing quietly, behaving soberly, and forgoing all forms of entertainment.

After the intensity of the previous week, the first wakeful moment on Easter Sunday morning was a delicious experience. From mourning to celebration, sobriety to exuberance, constant prayer to lazy recreation: what an overnight transformation! Best of all, though, was the prospect of going home the next day for a break of almost two weeks. Easter Sunday was the last full day of term, and after another absence of almost three months, we would be reunited again with our families.

The fact that we spent Easter away from home was symbolic in two different respects. It emphasized the religious significance of this feast over the secular—the Easter eggs and chocolates and big dinner we would otherwise have enjoyed with our families that day—and reminded us that our commitment to the Church had to take precedence over our commitment to our families. As such it was another example of those sacrifices intended to prepare us for a life of self-denial as priests.

§

The reunion with my family on Easter Monday was every bit as joyous as it had been on Boxing Day. My mother was so delighted to have me back she barely had any comment on my school report, with its news that I had failed to finish first in the end-of-term exams. "Never mind, never mind—you'll do better next time."

As the day unfolded I quickly became aware of a major cultural development that had completely passed us by in the seminary. My older brother could not stop talking about a new pop group from Liverpool that the whole country was raving about; he was totally incredulous that I had never even heard of them. Because of our isolation at Upholland, we seemed to be just about the only people in the country who did not know who the Beatles were. *Please Please Me* had reached the top of the charts in February, and the just-released *From Me to You* was zooming towards the same position. This had all escaped us at Upholland; since we didn't know these singles existed, none of the house record clubs had tried to buy them.

After seeing my brother's enthusiasm I was keen to hear the Beatles for myself, but had no chance of doing so at home. My parents were much less enthusiastic about this latest craze than the rest of the country, despite the Beatles' connection to Liverpool, and would not allow us to buy their records. Fortunately my brother's best friend had both the *Please Please Me* LP and the new single, and we spent a good part of our Easter break over at his house listening to them. While we certainly enjoyed the music, a big part of our excitement was the very idea that four blokes from our home city were attracting such attention. They made us proud to be Liverpudlians.

SUMMER TERM

Bad news travels fast, so the saying goes, and that was certainly true among the returning seminarians who converged on Upholland for the start of the summer term. No sooner had we shared our excitement over our late discovery of the Beatles than we learned they had been banned! The College authorities considered the lyrics of *Please Please Me* to be too suggestive. Given our ignorance of boy-girl relationships we were mystified; the ban made us search for meanings that would never otherwise have occurred to us. In any case it came too late: most of us had listened to the song so many times over the Easter break we knew the words by heart. Regardless, we would now have to wait another three months before hearing the Beatles again. Our dismay knew no bounds.

§

Five weeks into the term we had a much more serious reason for dismay. On June 3 we were stunned by the news that Pope John XXIII had died. All of us had been brought up to idolize whomever was Pope, and John XXIII had made this particularly easy to do. His warm, avuncular manner endeared him to Catholics and non-Catholics alike, and in less than five years he had come to personify the Papacy. It was hard to imagine anyone else bearing the title.

As the College of Cardinals began its work to elect a successor, Upholland also conducted a vital piece of ecclesiastical business: the ordination of a new crop of priests. In keeping with tradition this took place on the day before "Trinity Sunday," so named because it was the Feast of the Holy Trinity. In 1963 this fell on June 8, just five days after the Pope's death.

Archbishop Heenan was back with us once again to officiate, this time over an unusually long ceremony. What made the event so long was that there were ordinations to every single one of the minor and major orders. Ordinations to the lesser orders were always part of the Trinity ceremony, but it was unusual for this to include all three of the major orders; the diaconate was usually conferred in September. This year, however, one of the graduating senior seminarians was still a sub-deacon at the start of the day, and had to be elevated to the diaconate first. When he then joined the other deacons for the final phase of the proceedings, no fewer than fourteen men stood on the sanctuary awaiting ordination to the priesthood. Shortly afterwards they were lying face down on the floor rather than standing, as they took part in the ritual known as the "prostration," which signified their unworthiness for the office they were about to assume. Then came the most dramatic part of the ceremony, the solemn "imposition of hands." One by one, each deacon knelt in front of the Archbishop, who laid his hands on the man's head while uttering an invocation to the Holy Spirit. This was the single moment the ordinand had been working towards for much of his life: the moment he actually became a priest.

Once the ceremony was over there was great joy all around, not only among the new priests but also throughout the College. This, after all, was the reason we were all there.

Only ten of the fourteen priests ordained that day were for the Liverpool Archdiocese. Upholland also accepted senior seminarians from other Northern dioceses, and sometimes from even further afield. The graduating class in 1963 included new priests for Salford, Lancaster, and Nottingham, while the ordinands to lesser orders included men from Brentwood, Portsmouth, and— most distant of all—Kingston, Jamaica.

§

Had I known what was happening twenty miles away in Liverpool, my own mood on Ordination Day would have been a lot less cheerful. My grandmother died that day. She was the only one of my grandparents I had ever known, and I had always loved visiting her. The adventure of the bus ride, the delight she showed at seeing us, the stories she told us about our mother, the Cheesettes she invariably served—every aspect of our visits was memorable. Now she was gone.

Her death came as more of a shock because I had not realized how ill she was. My parents had written to let me know that she was in hospital, but without any more detail. And because of our isolation at Upholland, real-time communication about her illness was not possible. Indeed, I did not find out she had died until two days after she passed away, when Fr. Shaw took me aside after supper to tell me that my parents had just called with the news. Why they waited that long to call I will never know; perhaps they needed time to compose their thoughts about how I should be informed.

§

My own sad news notwithstanding, Upholland's celebratory season continued with Reunion Day. By tradition this took place on the Tuesday after Ordination Day, with priests from around the Archdiocese converging on their *alma mater* for its annual reunion. The day was always a holiday for the entire seminary, and while my first experience of the occasion may have been tinged with sadness, over the years it became one of my favorite days in the Upholland calendar. The atmosphere was relaxed and festive, the Profs were all in a great mood, and the early-summer weather was often perfect while we watched the traditional cricket match between "Past" and "Present" senior seminarians.

The weather was certainly ideal on Reunion Day 1963, which perhaps explained why the Rector decided we should have the next day off as well— officially, in honor of the first visit to Upholland by Bishop Foley of Lancaster. And since the day after that was *Corpus Christi*, a holy day of obligation and therefore another holiday, we experienced a rare three-day respite from the routine of College life.

The interruptions to this routine just kept coming. The following week brought Sports Day, the inter-house athletics competition that was the final big event in the sporting calendar for the year. Under Fr. Shaw's direction the Quarry had been turned into a running track for the occasion, lanes neatly marked with whitewash lines on the grass. No fancy synthetic surface for us, or even cinders, just Nature's irregular carpet! To add to the challenge for the runners, the Quarry had a distinct slope and was too small to accommodate a full-sized oval; this resulted in a track that was about 280 yards in circumference, with relatively flat straights but notably sloping turns, one uphill and the other down. Races longer than 280 yards involved peculiar partial laps—slightly more than half an extra lap, for example, in the 440-yard race.

Proving that the prayers of priests and seminarians have no more influence over the weather than those of the laity, the sky slowly darkened as the morning progressed, bringing a persistent rain that forced an end to the proceedings shortly after noon. Fortunately the weather was fair again by Thursday afternoon, allowing Sports Day to resume in place of our usual sporting activities.

When the final race was over and the scores were tallied, Mayne had amassed a grand total of 89 points, 16 ahead of More. This meant we had won not only the Sports Day Cup but also the House Shield for the year. My own contribution had been negligible, but that did not stop me from feeling very proud.

§

On June 21, the day after Mayne's Sports Day triumph, news came from Rome that a new Pope had been elected. The Rector was so thrilled that he ran to the main chapel and rang the bell for a full fifteen minutes all by himself. A short time later the Papal flag was hoisted above the central tower in the south wing, and for the rest of the day the College was abuzz with the news. Sad though we were at the death of John XXIII, the thought of having a new Pope was exciting.

Nine days later the papal coronation took place in Rome. Paul VI was now Pope. We could not be there in body, nor could we even watch on television, but in spirit we were part of the enthusiastic crowd that filled St. Peter's Square to overflowing.

§

After the excitement of ordinations, Reunion Day, Sports Day and the Papal succession, it came as something of a shock to realize that final exams were almost upon us. Time for me to put aside the distractions of the last few weeks and get on with some serious revising! The expectations at home would be as high as ever, and I had some ground to make up after slipping in the previous term. Suffice it to say that when the exams were over and the results came out, I was satisfied with the report card I would be taking home.

As the year drifted to a close we had time for one last burst of excitement. On July 21, the last Saturday of term, the College received a visit from a Cardinal. The visitor was His Eminence Cardinal Gracias, Archbishop of Bombay, who was accompanied by Archbishop Heenan. To a seminary this was akin to receiving royalty.

Indeed, the reception we gave him reminded me of a visit the Queen had made to Liverpool when I was in primary school. On that occasion, the entire school had marched about half a mile to join the crowd lining the Queen's route, so that we could wave and cheer as her limousine went past. The throng had been several people deep, however, and all I had managed to see was a brief glimpse of the limousine's roof. On this occasion, the walk was shorter and the view much better: even with the whole College participating, the crowd was only one person deep as we lined the drive to cheer the Cardinal's arrival.

Over three hundred days had now passed since we first came up that driveway ourselves, without of course any fanfare or acclaim. For all but twenty-six of those days we had been isolated from our families. The end of the year could not come quickly enough. Four days later it finally did.

§

Our long academic year did at least entitle us to a late start the following year; we were not due back at Upholland until September 14. And we all intended to savor every day of the vacation just as much as was humanly possible.

In the event, the summer break was harder to enjoy than I had hoped. As she had during previous breaks, my mother insisted I attend Mass every day, which meant there was not a single morning during the entire summer when I was allowed to sleep late. She also insisted on Benediction every Sunday afternoon, which effectively killed the day's recreational possibilities.

The other challenge was finding friends to socialize with. The boys I'd known at St. Margaret Mary's had all moved on to new schools, and while they were happy to see me now and again, they spent most of their time with newer friends from their current schools. The alternative might have been to meet up with my classmates from Upholland, but they all lived in different parts of Liverpool, or even further afield. So I spent most of the summer hanging out again with my brother and his friend. This at least gave me plenty of opportunity to listen to the Beatles. *She Loves You* was released towards the end of August, and by the time I returned to Upholland a few weeks later I knew every word, guitar lick and drumbeat.

If there was irony in my admiration for a song about romantic love—an emotion I had supposedly renounced—then I was oblivious to it.

CHAPTER 4

BOYS (AND MEN) OF THE CLOTH: FOUR CENTURIES OF THE SEMINARY SYSTEM

Although Upholland itself was not founded until 1883, the seminary system to which it belonged dated back to the sixteenth century. The system was originally established in response to a major crisis in the Church, and for most of its existence was regarded as one of the key reforms that helped to resolve that crisis. How tragically ironic, then, that four centuries later it should be cast as the villain responsible for the next major crisis in the Church's history.

Curiously, the system's origins can be traced to a construction project, albeit a grandiose one: the rebuilding of St. Peter's Basilica in Rome. In 1505, Pope Julius II decided to tear down the original St. Peter's—then more than a thousand years old and in decrepit condition—and replace it with a church he was determined would be the most magnificent building in the whole of Christendom. A few years later, when the huge cost of this undertaking became apparent, his successor opted to fund it by granting "indulgences" to those who gave alms for the new edifice. An indulgence is a form of pardon that accelerates entry into Heaven after death, by reducing or eliminating the time that must be spent in Purgatory atoning for sins that have been confessed and forgiven, but for which punishment is still due. Although the exchange of pardon for alms was not supposed to be an outright sale, in practice it often was. And despite the unseemly nature of such transactions, in most cases no objections were raised; this method of fundraising had after all been in use since the time of the Crusades.

In 1517, however, when the new indulgence for St. Peter's was first offered in Germany, it did run into objections. An obscure priest-professor at the University of Wittenberg took great exception to the flagrantly mercenary tactics used to promote it, and to the gross distortions these represented of Church doctrine relating to penance and indulgences. In an effort to stop the indulgence trade, he preached against it to his congregation and protested to his bishop—in both cases to no avail. Undaunted, he then turned to his fellow theologians, challenging them to a debate on the issue. In accordance with the usual practice, he issued his challenge by writing a "disputation" in Latin laying out his position, and nailing this to the door of the local church, which served as the *de facto* bulletin board for the university. The document was entitled the *Disputation of Doctor Martin Luther on the Power and Efficacy of Indulgences.* And its author had just set in motion one of the biggest upheavals in the history of Western civilization: the Reformation.

The *95 Theses*, as Luther's disputation came to be known, promptly became the first document in history to "go viral"—by the standards of the time, at least. Printers in three different cities rushed out copies in the original Latin, and numerous editions soon followed in German. To a modern reader, the reason for its popularity is not immediately obvious, since it consists mainly of obscure musings on repentance, purgatory, Papal authority to remit penalties due to sin, and specific claims made by the indulgence peddlers.

What it also contained, however, were pungent criticisms of the Pope. These, much more than Luther's doctrinal scruples, must have resonated strongly with his readers. From princes to peasants, people at all levels of society were deeply discontented with the Church's excessive involvement in temporal matters, its endless demands for money, and the corruption among its clergy. The Pope was the all-powerful monarch of an ecclesiastical empire, constantly asserting his right to appoint local clerics and take a share of their income—which in turn came from local landowners and peasants. German princes had fought hard against levies from Rome several times in the preceding century, and could see another one coming as the Pope geared up for a new crusade against the Turks. Lower down the pecking order, German peasants had agitated against the local clergy, complaining of "oppression by tithes, dues, penalties, excommunication, and tolls." Their vexation was only increased by the baseness of the clergy they were supporting, many of whom were illiterate, immoral, barely familiar with Scripture, and incapable of preaching. And then along came Luther, challenging the Pope's authority and daring to criticize him. This was a cause they could support.

Perhaps emboldened by this support, perhaps embittered by the Church's efforts to silence him but not the indulgence peddlers, Luther became progressively more radical over the next several years. In 1520 he published three pamphlets that were much more revolutionary in content and aggressive in tone, arguing that the secular government should reform the Church because it had failed to do so itself, that there were not seven sacraments but only three, and that salvation is to be found in faith alone and is totally dependent upon God's grace. All were rallying cries for those who wanted to escape the yoke of Papal rule.

The Church's response was to excommunicate Luther, and to strong-arm the civil authorities into declaring him a heretic and outlaw. Forced into hiding, he now had time and reason to pour out yet further radical texts. By this point there was no going back; a schism within the Church was inevitable. The newly emerging Protestant religion was quickly adopted by nations and principalities anxious to secede from Papal domination. Europe was changed forever. Rome's quest to construct the most glorious church in Christendom had cost it much more than money; the most powerful Church in history would never again exert such control over Western civilization.

In a belated attempt to re-establish its primacy, the Church convened a General Council in the northern Italian city of Trent. The Council's first session was not until 1545, almost a quarter-century after Luther had been excommunicated—belated indeed! The delegates had two main goals: to clarify the doctrines disputed by Protestants, and to reform the Church practices that had caused so much discontent. These were complicated tasks that, with several interruptions due to political disputes, took almost twenty years to complete. Many of the most contentious reforms had to wait until the final years of the Council, which concluded in 1563. On July 15 of that year, a decree was issued that some historians consider the Council's most important achievement. *Cum Adolescentium Aetas* mandated that seminaries should be established for the training and education of the clergy. In a passage that set the tone within these institutions for centuries to come, the Council explained why it considered them so necessary:

> Wereas the age of youth, unless it be rightly trained, is prone to follow after the pleasures of the world; and unless it be formed, from its tender years, unto piety and religion, before habits of vice have taken possession of the whole man, it never will perfectly, and without the greatest, and well-nigh special, help of Almighty God, persevere in ecclesiastical discipline...

The decree went on to specify in great detail how piety and religion were to be instilled into youths of tender years, who were defined as "such as are at least twelve years old." Seminarians were to learn grammar, singing, "ecclesiastical computation," and other liberal arts; be instructed in sacred Scripture, ecclesiastical works, the homilies of saints, the administration of sacraments, and the forms of rites and ceremonies; and attend Mass every day, and confession at least once a month.

Reform of the clergy had been high on the agenda for the Council, and the delegates were highly pleased by what they had achieved. According to one contemporary account, "So universal was the satisfaction caused by this decree, that many prelates hesitated not to declare, that if no other good were to result from the labors of the Council, this alone would compensate to them for all their fatigues and sacrifices."

Despite this enthusiasm, adoption of the new decree was neither speedy nor universal. In Italy, for example, although many dioceses quickly established seminaries, the large centers of Genoa and Florence waited a century or more before doing do. In Spain, at least twenty new seminaries were founded in a spurt that began in 1565, but over half of all dioceses still did not have one almost a century later. In Germany and the Netherlands, progress beyond the first few seminaries was limited by war and the spread of Protestantism. War was also one of several issues that hindered progress in France, where only 16 of 108 dioceses had "Tridentine" seminaries by 1620 (the adjective comes from *Tridentum*, the Latin name for Trent).

In two other countries—those of most interest for this narrative—implementation of the Council's decree had to wait much longer. At the time the decree was passed, Catholicism was suppressed in England and had only just arrived in the land that would become the United States. Over two centuries would pass before either country saw its first seminary on home soil.

In the case of England, the phrase "home soil" is an important qualifier, because a seminary to train English priests did open shortly after the Council of Trent ended—but on foreign soil, across the Channel in what is now northern France. Ironically, the quick establishment of this institution was made possible by the very measures that suppressed Catholicism in England. When Elizabeth I came to the throne in 1558 and re-imposed Protestantism as the official religion of the land, many Catholic intellectuals from Oxford fled to the French town of Douai (then a part of the Spanish Netherlands). Ten years later, an English priest by the name of William Allen drew on this expatriate community to found one of the earliest Tridentine seminaries anywhere, which became known as the English College, Douai. Although the College's original aim was to train a cadre of learned priests who would be ready to re-establish Catholicism in England once circumstances permitted, in practice the new priests did not wait for those circumstances to arise, but returned almost immediately to England to minister to the needs of its Catholics.

Their success can be gauged from the specificity with which they were targeted by a new law passed in 1585. The *Act Against Jesuits and Seminarists* made it high treason for any Jesuit or "seminary priest" to stay in the country or enter it from abroad, or for any student to remain in a foreign seminary. The Act also made it a felony to shelter or assist any priest, or to know of a clergyman's location and not disclose it to authorities. And since treason and felonies were punishable by death, life became even more dangerous for both priests and laity.

Undeterred by this danger, "seminary priests" from the Douai College continued to return to England. So too did new priests from the English Colleges in Rome, Spain and Portugal that had been established using Douai as a model. Over the course of the next century, many of these priests met their death as martyrs. The Church recognizes 342 English Catholics as having died for their religion between 1534 and 1680, most of whom were members of the clergy—including 153 priests from Douai.

Although the executions ceased after 1680, much of the next century remained bleak for Catholics in England. In the late 1700s, however, their lot began to improve. The Papists Act of 1778 restored some of their basic civil rights, a further Act in 1782 allowed them to operate Catholic schools, and the Roman Catholic Relief Act of 1791 permitted them to practice their religion, albeit with certain restrictions. Most importantly, this last Act also removed the threat of prosecution for priests.

Just as the climate began to ease for priests in England, the opposite was happening in France, making life extremely difficult for the English College in Douai. First, in 1789, came the French Revolution, which stripped the Church of much of its power and property, placed the clergy under state control, and eventually made them targets for imprisonment and even death. Then, in 1793, came war between Britain and France, and the confiscation soon afterwards of all British property on French soil. Not only was the College forced into permanent closure, but the few remaining staff and students were thrown into prison, where they were held until March 1795.

This was not, however, the end of the Douai College story. With the new freedom enjoyed by Catholics in England, refugees from Douai were soon invited to form the first seminaries on English soil. Just a month after the English College closed, St. Edmund's College in Ware was founded with help from staff and students who had escaped from Douai. The following year, the northerners among the escapees left to start a seminary near Durham, which subsequently became Ushaw College. For the next two centuries, both institutions proudly proclaimed their heritage back to the original founding of the English College in Douai in 1568. (Neither, though, is a seminary any more. St. Edmund's said goodbye to its last seminarians in 1975 and became a co-educational Catholic boarding school; Ushaw continued as a seminary for several decades longer, but was forced to close permanently in 2011.)

At almost the same time these institutions were being established in England, so too was the first seminary in the United States. Like its English counterparts, the new American seminary owed a great deal to the strong Catholic tradition in France. The French Church may initially have struggled to implement *Cum Adolescentium Aetas* after the Council of Trent, but by the late 1700s, almost every diocese had its own seminary. This transformation was due in no small part to the work of the Sulpicians, a community of diocesan clergymen dedicated to the training of additional priests; their name came from St. Sulpice, the church in Paris where their founder had been pastor. And in 1791, four Sulpician priests arrived in Baltimore and opened St. Mary's seminary, which is still in operation today.

In both countries, the nineteenth century was a period of exciting but challenging growth for Catholicism. In England, the Catholic Emancipation Act of 1829 finally removed almost all restrictions on the Church, allowing it to rebuild the diocesan infrastructures that had been absent for centuries; in the US, the rapid growth in population and continuing westward expansion led to the establishment of numerous new dioceses. With this growth came a corresponding increase in the demand for new priests, and for new seminaries in which to train them.

Ecclesiastical authorities in both countries then struggled with a problem that had confronted many European dioceses ever since *Cum Adolescentium Aetas* was first promulgated: how to establish seminaries that were fully in conformance with the Tridentine ideal.

To borrow a phrase coined by one historian, perfect compliance with this ideal would require that seminarians be educated separately from other students "from boyhood to priesthood." In many dioceses, however, the number of candidates for the priesthood was simply too small to sustain the skilled faculty required to train them, particularly if a single institute had to provide both secondary and tertiary education. To be viable, many seminaries therefore had to accept lay students alongside those pursuing the priesthood, who were then more subject to worldly influence than the Council had wished. Even the prominent institutions mentioned above—Douai College, its successors at Ware and Ushaw, and St. Mary's in Baltimore—had to settle for this compromise. Moreover, relatively few seminaries hosted students all the way from adolescence to ordination; more typically, the secondary phase of education was provided in a minor seminary, with students transferring to a separate major seminary for the college-level study of philosophy and theology.

In spite of the logistical difficulties, the English and American hierarchies were determined to abide by the Tridentine decree to the extent they reasonably could. The presence of lay students was a bigger concern than the discontinuity between minor and major seminaries. In England, Provincial Synods in 1859 and 1873 passed resolutions calling for each bishop to do his best to establish a diocesan seminary in which "the Church students may be taught their philosophy and theology apart from intercourse with laics." In the US, the Third Plenary Council of Baltimore decreed that "Every diocese should, if possible, have its own major and minor seminary set apart exclusively for the education of ecclesiastical students. Where this is impossible, one higher and one preparatory seminary should be established in each province." The Council did, however, recognize that even this might be difficult, and so expressly permitted young men studying for the priesthood "to study their classics at secular colleges, wherever, owing to want of means, small or preparatory seminaries, which are exclusively for ecclesiastical students, cannot as yet be erected."

The history of the Upholland seminary illustrates both the challenge that dioceses faced and the vision to which they aspired. Its history is recounted in the book *Mitres & Missions in Lancashire* by Peter Doyle, an English academic who was a priest earlier in his career, and was in fact a history teacher and housemaster at Upholland when I arrived there. As he explains, when the English hierarchy was re-established in 1850 the new diocese of Liverpool took immediate steps to secure its future supply of priests. George Brown, the first bishop appointed to the new see, co-opted a recently established Catholic boarding school, St. Edward's College, as the diocesan minor seminary. Its re-designation did not, however, result in a sudden rush of ecclesiastical students, and for the next fifty years St. Edward's was obliged to educate lay pupils as well. But in the early 1900s, under the leadership of an authoritarian Rector known as Canon "Bunker" Banks, the College did finally become a pure Tridentine seminary, devoted solely to the education of future priests in strict isolation from the outside world.

Meanwhile, the third Bishop of Liverpool, Bernard O'Reilly, had taken to heart one of the key resolutions passed by the Provincial Synod in 1873, and pressed ahead with the establishment of a separate major seminary for the diocese. After several years of planning and fundraising, the foundation stone for the new institution was laid in 1880 at Walthew Park, just outside the village of Upholland; the site had been chosen for its remote location about twenty miles from the center of Liverpool, a distance which in that era was more than enough to secure isolation from the city's influence. Three years later, St. Joseph's College accepted its first students. Remarkably, of the thirty-one students in the initial intake, all but two were subsequently ordained. This success came in spite of the College's early struggles with a variety of financial, staffing and governance issues, which took more than a decade to resolve. Their resolution led to a period of relative stability that lasted until 1914, when the outbreak of the First World War made it impossible to ignore the demands of the outside world. As the War entered its final months in 1918 there were only ten students left at Upholland, a number that was reduced even further when four were ordained priests. The remaining six were transferred to the Ushaw seminary near Durham, and Upholland was converted into an orphanage.

This arrangement was only ever intended to be temporary, however, and when the College re-opened as a seminary in 1920 it was with a much bigger vision, perhaps befitting the elevation of the Liverpool diocese to archdiocesan status several years earlier. The major and minor seminaries were to be united in a single facility, isolated from the world, a true Tridentine institution. The old St. Edward's seminary had been closed the previous year and the building transferred to the Irish Christian Brothers, who re-opened it as a secondary school. The minor seminarians now took up residence in what had previously been the major seminary at Upholland, while construction began of three huge neo-Gothic wings that would form a quadrangle with the original building, and a matching chapel behind one corner of this quadrangle. By 1927, the work had progressed far enough to allow the senior students to return from their exile at other seminaries. Under the guidance of its new Rector, Monsignor Joseph Dean, Upholland then became a model Tridentine seminary.

Mgr. Dean was the epitome of strictness, committed to absolute doctrinal orthodoxy, severe discipline, and strict isolation from the outside world. The depth of his commitment is perfectly illustrated by the manner of his eventual departure. In 1942, he resigned on principle after his opposition to a small but humane relaxation of Tridentine discipline—allowing the minor seminarians a short break at home after Christmas—was overruled by a special commission appointed by the Archbishop, with his own staff also supporting the change.

In spite of his abrupt resignation, Mgr. Dean's influence was still much in evidence when I arrived at Upholland two decades later. Granted, we had breaks at both Christmas and Easter by then, but the regimen we followed was otherwise very close to the Tridentine ideal—as should be clear from the account in the previous chapter.

Nor was Upholland alone in its commitment to this ideal, as is very evident from several other accounts of seminary life, on both sides of the Atlantic. The most eloquent of these is John Cornwell's novelistic memoir, *Seminary Boy*, in which he describes life during the 1950s at Cotton College, the minor seminary for the archdiocese of Birmingham. Cotton was even more remote than Upholland and, from Cornwell's account, just as strictly Tridentine (with the exception that it did not also house the diocesan major seminary, as Upholland did).

Two other highly articulate accounts of seminary life in about the same period also exist, both set in the US. But before we consider the similarities between the institutions they describe and those at Upholland and Cotton, it will be useful to highlight a few important differences that had developed between the seminary systems in the two countries.

By the mid 1950s the American system had grown much larger than its English counterpart, in keeping with the greater size of the Catholic population. At that time there were thirty-three million Catholics in the US and only three million in England; this ratio was reflected in the number of diocesan seminaries in the two countries, seventy-one and nine respectively. The US also had a large number of what the *Official Catholic Directory* called "novitiates and scholasticates"—essentially, seminaries for religious orders. The 1953 *Directory*, for example, noted that there were 17,258 students in 368 such institutions—almost two thousand more students than in the seventy-one diocesan seminaries. In England, by comparison, there were only three non-diocesan seminaries.

The American and English systems were also organized somewhat differently, reflecting local differences in the approach to post-primary education more generally. College-bound students in England, for example, typically receive all seven years of their secondary education in the same school, whereas American students spend three years in middle school and then four in high school. Accordingly, English minor seminaries accepted students at age eleven and educated them for the next seven years, whereas American minor seminaries only covered the four high-school years, with students entering at age fourteen after attending secular middle schools.

Whereas attendance at a minor seminary was not an absolute requirement on the path to the priesthood—in spite of the Council of Trent's preference for clerical training to begin at a young age—the adult stages of this training were mandatory for all aspiring priests. And like the earlier stages, their organization in the two countries reflected local educational norms. In England, where a bachelor's degree can be earned in three years and a doctorate in three more, future priests spent six years in a major seminary studying philosophy and theology before ordination. In the US, by contrast, where bachelor's and doctoral degrees each normally require at least four years of study, the major-seminary phase of training lasted for eight years—four in a "college seminary," followed by four in a "theologate."

In total, therefore, the training period for an American priest ranged between eight and twelve years, the latter only if he entered a high-school seminary at the age of fourteen; in England, the range was between six and thirteen years, the latter for priests who had started as minor seminarians at the age of eleven.

Back, then, to those two accounts of life in American seminaries that were mentioned above. Both cover the period between the late 1950s and early 1960s. One, *Married to the Church* by Raymond Hedin, describes life in St. Francis seminary in Milwaukee, Wisconsin (where, coincidentally, I also lived for an extended period three decades later). The other, *Seminary: A Search* by Paul Hendrickson, recalls the years he spent at Holy Trinity Seminary in Alabama, the training institute for a tiny order of missionary priests. Both authors entered their respective seminaries at the age of fourteen, and although neither went on to become a priest, each produced a memoir decades later in which he combined his own retrospective view of seminary life with those of former classmates.

And as their accounts make clear, whatever differences there may have been in the size and organization of the American seminary system, it was just as committed as its English counterpart to the Tridentine ideal of isolating trainee priests from the outside world. Among former seminarians at St. Francis, the verdict was that "they put a fence around the seminary and kept you inside. They controlled all of our information." These sentiments were echoed by men who had attended Holy Trinity, who concluded that "[t]here was far too much protection: we were far too isolated."

Former students are not the only ones to have remarked upon the isolationism of seminaries during this period. Fr. Howard Bleichner is the former Rector of two prestigious US seminaries and an acknowledged leader in American priestly formation. In his recent book about the rapidly changing priesthood, *View from the Altar*, he observes that:

> Seminaries were usually constructed in secluded locations, the better to underscore that they represented a world apart, indeed, a world unto themselves... Seminarians were rarely permitted to leave the grounds, and only with explicit permission. From a sociological point of view, seminaries have regularly been compared to minimum security prisons...
>
> The seminary deliberately cultivated the quality of an igloo, a place frozen in time... The outside world had little impact on and no point of entry to this self-enclosed world. In the official chronicles of St. Mary's Seminary, Baltimore, which stretch back to 1791, there is not a single reference to the Civil War.

These observations relate to the seminary system as it existed before the Second Vatican Council, which ushered in reforms that Fr. Bleichner, like the National Review Board, believes were significant contributors to the clergy sexual abuse crisis. The true impact of these reforms will be debated in a later chapter; for the moment, however, we can safely conclude that prior to their introduction, the American seminary system continued to adhere closely to the precepts laid down by the Council of Trent.

In one respect, the continuing loyalty to these precepts on both sides of the Atlantic is surprising. Effectively, it meant that papal advice was being ignored. A dozen years before Vatican II convened, Pope Pius XII had advocated some relaxation of the strict isolation and monastic discipline that were characteristic of Tridentine seminaries. In his 1950 "Apostolic Exhortation" *Menti nostrae*, instructing "the clergy of the entire world" about their role in post-war society, the Pope had written:

> In the first place, it is necessary to remember that pupils in minor seminaries are adolescents separated from the natural environment of their home. It is necessary, therefore, that the life the boys lead in the seminaries correspond as far as possible to the normal life of boys...
>
> If young men—especially those who have entered the seminary at a tender age are educated in an environment too isolated from the world, they may, on leaving the seminary, find serious difficulty in their relations with either the ordinary people or the educated laity, and it may happen that they either adopt a misguided and false attitude toward the faithful or that they consider their training in an unfavorable light. For this reason, it is necessary that the students come in closer contact, gradually and prudently, with the judgments and tastes of the people in order that when they... begin their ministry they will not feel themselves disorientated...

Upholland, clearly, had paid little heed to this advice by the time I arrived in 1962. The life described in the previous chapter could hardly be said to "correspond... to the normal life of boys"; rather, it represented exactly what Pius XII had warned against, namely education "in an environment too isolated from the world." To judge from the accounts of John Cornwell, Raymond Hedin and Paul Hendrickson, all of whom were seminarians some years after *Menti nostrae* was issued, the institutions they attended also ignored the Pope's advice. So too, it seems, did the seminaries familiar to Fr. Bleichner, who was ordained in 1967, and would therefore have begun his training in the late 1950s.

The decision of all these seminaries not to follow Pius XII's guidance presumably reflected general satisfaction with the *status quo*. Indeed, when the Catholic historian, Monsignor Philip Hughes, published *A Popular History of the Reformation* in 1957, he could hardly have praised the seminary system more highly, describing it as the one legacy from the Council of Trent that "more than anything else, has made all the difference between the health of the Church in the last four centuries and its chronic state in the Middle Ages."

The confidence of seminaries in the *status quo* must also have been reinforced by the strong growth in enrolment they experienced during the 1950s. By the end of the decade, the total seminary population in the US was almost 50 percent higher than it had been at the start; at Upholland, the number of new students in 1960 was more than double the number in 1950. On both sides of the

Atlantic, seminaries may simply have interpreted their booming enrolment as a measure of success and concluded that no changes were needed.

What none of them realized at the time, however, was that by a far more important metric, the seminary system was failing abysmally: between 1950 and 1960, the incidence of child molestation by American priests increased over six-fold. To understand why this happened, we will need to learn more about the impact of the seminary environment on its students, and about the factors that cause adults to abuse children. Such will be the work of the next two chapters.

CHAPTER 5

TRANQUILITY, THEN TURMOIL: UPHOLLAND COLLEGE, 1963-65

Without question, my second year at Upholland was the happiest. The peculiar routine of seminary life now felt familiar, my relationships with my classmates were mostly good, and puberty had not yet arrived to torment me about my intended vocation. The long hours in chapel felt less like obligations and more like opportunities for prayer; I was as devout and committed to the priesthood as I would ever be.

My own mood was undoubtedly helped by the overall mood of optimism within the College and the Church. In the College's case this found expression (literally) in concrete form, with the start of construction work on a new wing, the seminary's response to overcrowding caused by several years of high enrolment. In the Church's case the optimism was generated by the Second Vatican Council, in session once again in Rome. Late in October we were the grateful beneficiaries of one the Council's early reforms, when the Epistle and the Gospel at Mass were read in English for the very first time. Sitting in chapel at the crack of dawn, barely awake, we certainly appreciated the change; uninterrupted Latin day after day was a big challenge to our powers of concentration, and even two short bursts of English made a significant difference.

The positive tone of the year was briefly dispelled by a shattering event in late November: the assassination of President Kennedy. On this occasion there was no question of insulating us from the outside world, as we had been during the Cuban Missile Crisis a year earlier; the Rector was so upset that he broke protocol to inform the entire seminary. During supper on the evening of November 22 he hurried into the junior refectory, threw open the connecting doors to the senior refectory—the only time I can ever recall them being opened—and stunned us with the news from Dallas. Like Catholics everywhere we felt the shock of Kennedy's assassination particularly deeply; even in his lifetime, he was an almost mythical hero to us, a Catholic who had managed to ascend to the most powerful office in the world. Outside of retreat, I cannot remember a more subdued evening at Upholland.

Slowly, though, the positive atmosphere returned. First came Christmas, as joyous as its predecessor, then a winter as mild as the previous one had been brutal. Even Lent did not seem quite so bleak as usual, thanks to an unexpected decision from the newly promoted headmaster, Fr. Cheetham: impressed by the lyrics of *Can't Buy Me Love*, he lifted the College's ban on Beatles' music. And then, one week into the summer term, came the biggest boost of all, at least for the Liverpool fans among us. By thrashing Arsenal 5-0 on April 18, the Reds secured their first League title in almost twenty years. Life was good. How could I not be happy? And indeed I was—in my conscious mind at least.

Given what happened the following year, however, I can look back now and identify clear signs of trouble to come, all stemming from my failure to adjust fully to life without the emotional support of my family. Unaware of my subconscious reason for doing so, I still used silly wordplays as a way to draw attention to myself. Most of the time these were harmless, but sometimes they amounted to jokes at other people's expense, which I failed to recognize in my rush to fire off a witty line. Perhaps because of this, or perhaps because my academic ranking made them less inclined to forgive my silliness, some of my classmates began to show impatience with my behavior. One or two began to make fun of me over a speech impediment I had never been able to conquer: my inability to pronounce the letter "r," which from my lips always emerged as "w." For the moment their teasing was still relatively mild—mimicry and laughter at my mispronunciations. Over time, though, it would become more intense, largely (I would now suppose) in retaliation for my own unchanged behavior. And when that happened, as we shall shortly see, my response was truly extraordinary.

§

If Low Figures was the high point of my time at Upholland, High Figures was the low. Perhaps I was being punished for my obsession with silly wordplays.

The year began smoothly enough, my classmates and I relishing our new status as the most senior boys in the Lower Line. A few more friends had left and the completion of the new wing had been delayed, but these were minor disappointments compared with the advantages of seniority. In my case, for example, these included the fulfillment of my long-held ambition to play for the Mayne house football team. My selection was a tribute more to my size than my skills—by now there were only about twenty boys in the house and I was one of the biggest—but I still thoroughly enjoyed the experience, even more so because we won both of our first-term games.

Unfortunately for my peace of mind, the physical development that secured my place on the house football team had other, highly troubling, consequences. Puberty was upon me. And as this gradually transformed my body, it also created the first real difficulties I had ever experienced in complying with the moral dictates of the Church.

Up until now, being "good" had required relatively little effort. As the easygoing third child in a large Catholic family, I had no particular reason or inclination to dishonor God, the Sabbath or my parents; to steal or kill; to tell more than the occasional lie; or to show any untoward interest in my neighbor's wife or possessions. Avoiding sin, especially serious sin, really did not require that much work on my part.

Now, all of a sudden, my mind was frequently beset with "impure thoughts" and, worse still, the fierce temptation to engage in "impure deeds." Resisting these thoughts and temptations was a continual struggle, but one I absolutely needed to win, because capitulation would be a sin. And not just some minor infraction but a mortal sin, sufficient to condemn me to an eternity in Hell were I to die before confessing it. In a matter of months I went from moral tranquility to spiritual turmoil; my conscience ached from the sheer effort of policing my thoughts all the time.

In theory, the challenges posed by sexual maturity should have been no worse for me than for any other Catholic boy of the same age. Seminarian or not, everyone was supposed to resist the promptings of the flesh. In practice, however, I suspect that I and my fellow seminarians took the obligation of complete "purity" much more seriously than our secular counterparts. They, after all, had every reason to expect that sexual activity would be an integral part of their future lives, whereas we expected to banish it completely from ours; indeed, failure to do so would preclude us from pursuing our chosen vocation.

Sadly, as we now know, that last statement is not true as it should be. In countries all around the globe, seminarians who should have been precluded from pursuing their vocations were not; after ordination they failed in the worst possible way to banish sexual activity from their lives, engaging in acts of abuse against children. And as I will argue in a later chapter, their heinous behavior as adults may have been caused in part by their struggles as adolescents against sins of impurity.

§

Perhaps because their hormones were raging too, some of my classmates gradually became less tolerant of my exaggerated puns and silly wordplays. The ribbing that had started the previous year over my speech defect now turned more serious, with two or three boys constantly tormenting me. My adversaries even came up with a name for my impediment, which they called a "taunt." For weeks after coining this term, the ringleaders would break into a chant of "Miles has got a taunt, Miles has got a taunt" whenever they saw me, whether I was annoying them or not at the time.

Early in the second term, as the "taunt" campaign continued, my sinking morale took a further blow. My two best friends suddenly decided to drop me. In retrospect and with the eyes of a parent, I now see this as fairly normal behavior for early teenagers; my own children went through similar experiences in middle school. My erstwhile friends may simply have been following the lead of their peers—it was certainly not fashionable at the time to side with me. But whatever their reasons, I was devastated. By the end of January I felt totally miserable, isolated from home without a friend in the world. Decades later I still vividly recall an agitated walk on the Quarry, all by myself, feeling cast out, misunderstood and completely alone.

Only when writing this memoir did I see for the first time a connection between my feelings that day and an astonishing deception I committed shortly afterwards. As on previous occasions, my reaction to unhappiness was a dramatic but subconscious ploy for attention. This time, however, I far surpassed my previous performances.

The big deception began with news of another boy's illness. Who he was, I can no longer recall; what mattered was that he had been rushed to hospital to "have an operation" for appendicitis. That phrase was crucial. From my mother's proud accounts of her own surgeries I knew that "having an operation" made you a very special patient, guaranteed to receive solicitous attention from numerous members of the medical profession. And from my fellow seminarian's illness, I now knew of one condition certain to secure such attention: appendicitis. I had absolutely no idea what this was, but immediately began to fantasize about developing it and being rushed to hospital myself. An operation! For me! That would make *me* the focus of everyone's attention!

After talking with other boys who knew the recent victim, I quickly identified an easy route to convert my fantasy into reality. His primary symptom, I learned, had been a sharp pain in the lower right-hand side of the abdomen. Once I heard this, the next step was inevitable and irresistible. A few days later, I presented myself in the Surgery complaining of just such a pain. Without too much inquiry I was sent to the Sick Bay and the doctor summoned. His examination could easily have brought a quick end to the matter, not least because I was still rather vague about the exact location of my appendix, and therefore of my supposed pain. His approach to examining me must have tipped me off, however, because I was able to grimace at just the right moment when he probed my abdomen for tenderness.

Even so, the initial reward for my improvisation was disappointing: continued confinement in the Sick Bay for observation, and a liquid diet consisting of soup and Bovril. Yuck! This was not the dramatic evacuation to hospital I had envisaged. But if a protracted display of symptoms was what it would take to get me my operation, I was up for the challenge. The doctor returned at regular intervals over the next several weeks to examine me, and despite the awful diet and the boredom of my confinement, I never once relented in complaining of pain in my lower right abdomen.

My determination finally brought me the reward I was seeking. After I had been in the Sick Bay over a month, the doctor sent me to a hospital in St. Helens for examination by a specialist. My weeks of rehearsal with the doctor must have enabled me to give a command performance for the specialist, because he declared that I had a "grumbling appendix" and that it should be removed. A day or two later I was admitted to the men's surgical ward, and shortly thereafter relieved of my appendix. The surgeon may have been perplexed to discover the complete absence of any inflammation in the tissue he removed, but if he voiced any doubts about my "illness," nobody ever said so to me.

Back in 1965, when all of this occurred, hospitals were not in a mad rush to discharge their patients, so I spent ten days or so in the men's ward recovering from the surgery. Ironically, for the first time in this whole saga I was now in genuine pain, from the six-inch incision the army-trained surgeon had made. (Some of my eight stitches left bigger scars than would now be left by the entire procedure).

More daunting than the pain, however, was the circumstance of being the only young teenager in a ward full of grown men. From time to time some of the men would try to engage me in conversation about my school, but I was determined to say at little as possible. Given all their swearing and their ribald banter with the nurses, I was afraid they would poke fun at me for being a seminarian. When I first arrived on the ward I found their conversations quite shocking, because I had never previously been exposed to much profanity or vulgarity. By the end of my stay, however, I was as fascinated as I was shocked, particularly by the coquettish responses from some of the pretty young nurses.

After being released from the hospital I spent several additional weeks at home recuperating, by which time the Easter vacation had started. When this was over and I finally returned to Upholland, I had been out of the classroom for over three months and missed almost an entire term.

Looking back on this saga I am appalled at what I did, but also amazed at the detachment I felt throughout the whole episode. Most people would assume that a fourteen-year old boy who behaved as I did, faking appendicitis for weeks until hospitalized and cut open, must be seriously disturbed. But that is not how I felt at the time, nor (I think) how anyone at Upholland would have described me. As far as I can remember, the rest of my behavior during this period was perfectly normal. Having identified a way to address the deep unhappiness I was feeling—without realizing that this was what I was doing—I simply moved ahead calmly with implementation, never questioning my course of action, and never letting it affect the rest of my behavior. At no point after I first complained of my imaginary pain did I seriously consider dropping the pretence, which became such a part of me that over time I almost came to believe it myself. Indeed, if the subject of my operation ever came up in later years, I would barely remember as I told the story that my "appendicitis" was completely fabricated, and certainly never mentioned this fact to anyone else. This chapter is the first accurate account I have ever given.

Despite the calmness I displayed throughout my supposed illness, in retrospect I can only conclude (as I suggested above most other people would) that I must have been seriously disturbed at the time. The daily struggle with salacious thoughts, the desertion by my best friends, the merciless teasing by my adversaries, the long separations from home—all combined to traumatize me during a period that would have been difficult enough without unusual stresses, early adolescence. I say this not to garner belated sympathy, but because of its potential relevance to the wider issue of sexual abuse by priests—a connection that will be explored in some detail later.

§

Fortunately, the appendicitis episode marked the low point of my life at Upholland. A week or two into the summer term it was clear that the friction with my classmates had dissipated, and we were all back on friendly terms. From this point forward I can recall no further incidents of unusually needy behavior or excessively annoying semantics on my part. By some strange irony, the treatment I received for my diagnosed (but phony) physical ailment turned out to be just what I had needed for my undiagnosed (but real) psychological ailment—a pathological craving for attention. Perhaps the nursing I received was enough to heal my sense of neglect. Perhaps also I was growing up. And perhaps the "taunt" campaign helped me too, by finally teaching me to recognize when I was annoying other people.

One lesson this campaign definitely taught me was the importance of correcting my pronunciation of the letter "r." When the year was over and I was back at home for the summer vacation, I spent many hours experimenting with different ways of moving my tongue against my teeth, until finally I found one that reproducibly resulted in the right rendition—a phrase I could now even say correctly! (Although it might potentially have been regarded as annoying word play…)

While my relationships and elocution proved relatively easy to fix, the other issue that had precipitated my crisis was much less tractable. Puberty was irreversible. Sexual thoughts and impulses were here to stay. The daily battle between my conscience and my physiology continued to rage. As yet I did not allow this to deter me from the priesthood; I prayed a lot, and assumed that I would somehow be able to tough my way through a difficult period. But in looking ahead, I was beginning to recognize the enormity of the challenge that celibacy would pose if I stayed the course.

§

When we returned to Upholland in September 1965 we had moved up to the Higher Line, where we would spend the final four of our seven years in the minor seminary. In concept, this was the equivalent of moving up from middle to high school in the US. And in practice, the Higher Line felt so different that it was almost as though we had in fact moved to a new school.

The differences were apparent right from the start of each day. The first sound we heard was still the raucous clamor of a football rattle, but this now jolted us awake at six, half an hour earlier than we were used to. The extra time we gained was spent in chapel, where seven o'clock Mass was now preceded by thirty minutes of meditation. And instead of being by ourselves in the Lower Line chapel, we were with the Upper House in the main chapel—the location henceforth for all of our devotional activities. After Mass, as previously, we returned to our dormitory to make our beds before breakfast. This year, however, the dormitory in question was in the Higher Line wing on the north side of the Quad. So too were most of our other facilities, including the classroom to which we made our way after breakfast.

Once there, we faced a more serious program of study than before, as we launched into the two-year curriculum for GCE "O-levels." Most of us would be taking eight or nine of these public exams at the end of the following year, so we had a lot of material to cover.

Outside of the classrooms our social lives were still centered around "houses," but these were different too: Arrowsmith, Barlow and Campion, named after three more of the English martyrs. Since the housemasters already knew our sporting capabilities, there was no need for tryouts like those we had in the Lower Line. I had been assigned to Campion.

In one respect our houses now played an even bigger part in daily life than before, because the Higher Line common rooms were organized by house rather than by class, as they had been in the Lower Line. We therefore spent much of our leisure time with fellow house-members rather than classmates.

The common rooms also had one major amenity we had not previously been allowed: newspapers and magazines. The main attraction of these was the sports pages, not the news coverage, which was of interest only if it happened to include a story about the Beatles. Our access to music was also improved, since the house record collections were kept in the common rooms rather than the housemasters'. Inevitably, the record we played most during the first few weeks of term was the latest offering from the Beatles: the *Help!* LP that had been released with the movie that summer.

The final change in our daily routine was that we went to bed later. The bell for night prayers sounded at ten past nine rather than eight-thirty, and by the time prayers were over and we had made our way via the washrooms to the dormitory, lights-out typically did not occur until about ten o'clock. In silence, of course—*magnum silentium* was still the rule.

§

After lording it over the Lower Line for a year, we now had to adjust to being back at the bottom of the pecking order, the youngest boys in the Higher Line. At least we could resume our acquaintance with the boys in the two classes above us, whom we had known when we first arrived at Upholland; after they had moved up to the Higher Line ahead of us, the ban on conversation between the Lines had forced us to ignore them.

Together with *magnum silentium*, this ban had a purpose we were just beginning to understand—and it was not what we had been told when we first arrived in Underlow. Back then, the story had been that these rules would teach us the virtue of obedience, a necessary component of priestly self-discipline. While this may have been true, as we grew older we suspected that they had another purpose, which was to minimize any opportunities for sexually mature older boys and senior seminarians to prey on younger boys, or for illicit liaisons between students of similar age.

As I can attest, unfortunately, if their purpose was to protect boys against unwanted sexual advances, these rules were not completely effective. My ascent into the Higher Line had put me once more within the circle of an older boy who had previously made lewd remarks to me. He now resumed. For a while that was as far as he went, until one day during an excursion to the local swimming pool he tried to grope my genitals under cover of the water. I pushed him away and kicked out furiously, and that was the end of the incident. He never again tried anything similar, but the mere sight of him was always enough to put me on edge.

Compared with the thousands of cases of sexual abuse by the clergy that have emerged in recent years, what happened to me was very mild, more a case of sexual harassment than abuse. The would-be abuser did not get very far, but much more importantly, was not a priest. This spared me from having to deal with the spiritual trauma experienced by many victims of the clergy, who were shaken to the core not just by the abuse itself but by the identity of the perpetrator—in their eyes the trusted representative of both God and His Church.

The attempt to molest me was nonetheless highly distressing, and certainly added to the major discomfort I already felt about sex because of my continual struggle with impure thoughts. The mind-control skills I had learned from that struggle—how to quickly corral unwanted thoughts and divert my attention to safer subjects—helped me to avoid thinking too much about what had happened. Within a surprisingly short time I had walled up the incident in a safe compartment somewhere in the recesses of my mind. The only noticeable vestiges were a sense of unease whenever I saw the would-be molester, and the occasional nightmare (sometimes years later) about being molested. In the grand scheme of things these were minor wounds that have long since healed; until the publicity in recent years about the clergy sexual abuse scandals, I had barely thought about the incident in decades.

For this account, the episode's larger significance may lie in the fact that nobody else knew about it except me and the perpetrator. I certainly never told anyone, and can safely assume that he didn't either. Clearly, if I could be the subject of sexual advances without anyone else being aware of the fact, it's quite possible that other boys were too, and that there was more sexual misconduct— or indeed consensual sexual activity—at Upholland than I ever realized. Perhaps naïvely, I had always thought that any sexual activity at the College was limited to solo acts in private. But from recent correspondence with former students who were near-contemporaries of mine, I gather this may not have been the case.

If in fact other boys were molested at Upholland, and the same was true at minor seminaries elsewhere, this could help to explain at least some of the abusive behavior by priests; in general, child molesters are more likely than non-molesters to have been victims of sexual abuse themselves.

Many other factors may also contribute to the development of abusive behavior. And as we shall now see, several of these appear to correspond to aspects of the seminary environment I have been describing.

CHAPTER 6

DESCENT INTO EVIL:
HOW PRIESTS BECAME ABUSERS

Having explored seminary life in some detail, we can now return to the important question posed in the Preface: Why exactly did seminaries predispose so many priests to molest children? To address this question we will first review current scientific thinking about abusive behavior in general, and then consider how this might apply to priests in particular.

Given the huge harm done to so many victims by predatory priests, some readers may find the discussion that follows distasteful; in seeking to identify developmental experiences that could have predisposed these men to commit abuse, it may seem like an attempt to excuse their behavior. That is absolutely not the intention. Such behavior was, is and always will be inexcusable. The sole purpose of this chapter is to understand what may have caused priests to act as they did, so that such actions can be prevented in the future.

CAUSES OF ABUSIVE BEHAVIOR

The first step in understanding why priests molested children is to ask why any male, priest or not, engages in such behavior. This is not an easy question to answer. Cause and effect are often difficult to prove in science, but especially so in the behavioral sciences. If a researcher in the natural sciences wants to demonstrate that X causes Y, he or she can usually conduct experiments in which circumstances including X are created, and the impact on Y is then measured; to confirm that any change in Y is indeed caused by X and not some other factor, the results are compared with those obtained when the same procedure is conducted in the absence of X, or in the presence of other potential causes of Y. Although such prospective experiments are sometimes possible in the behavioral sciences, their scope is necessarily more limited; clearly, when the behavior under study is harmful, no experiment can be performed that might actually induce it.

This point is well illustrated by the investigations that have been conducted into the causes of sexually abusive behavior by adults towards children. Physiological experiments have demonstrated that male pedophiles experience greater sexual arousal in response to pictures of children than to pictures of adults, whereas the opposite is true for non-pedophiles. By itself, however, this observation is not sufficient to explain why pedophiles molest children, and any experiment that tried to establish a causal connection would be unthinkable. Instead, researchers must make detailed retrospective assessments of adults who have abused children, searching for specific experiences and personality traits that are more common among these molesters than among comparable non-molesters. Unless a particular factor correlates extremely highly with abusive behavior, its role in the development of such behavior must be considered an inference rather than a firm conclusion. And for most of the factors that have been evaluated as potential causes of abusive behavior, the correlation is not particularly strong. Given the complexity of human nature, the spectrum of abusive behaviors that occur, and the small numbers of abusers typically available for such studies, this is not really surprising: in most cases, multiple factors will contribute to a particular individual becoming a child molester, and the combination that sends one person down this path may be very different from the combination that sends another.

Faced with this complexity, in the early 1980s Dr. David Finkelhor carefully reviewed the numerous theories that had been proposed to explain abusive behavior, and categorized them into four main groups according to the nature of the issue each was trying to address. Thus the majority of theories attempted to answer one of four key questions (stated here assuming the abuser is a male, which is almost always the case): What makes a man capable of being sexually aroused by a child? Why does he derive emotional satisfaction from relating sexually to a child? What prevents him from seeking sexual gratification with other adults? And why do the usual taboos not deter him from engaging in sexual relations with children?

Having recognized that these were the key issues underlying multiple different theories, Dr. Finkelhor then proposed a multi-factorial model to explain why adults molest children. According to this model, four factors must be in place for an adult to engage (and continue to engage) in abusive behavior: sexual arousal, emotional congruence, blockage and disinhibition. As will be appreciated, the names given to these factors are also concise summaries of the four issues highlighted above.

(Somewhat confusingly, another theoretical framework developed by Dr. Finkelhor is also referred to by some authors as his "four-factor model." Whereas the model just described seeks to explain *why* adults molest children, the second model focuses on *how* acts of sexual abuse actually occur. Two of the four "pre-conditions" it postulates cover the same ground as the four factors noted above, while the others relate more to the abuser's *modus operandi*—how he overcomes potential deterrents and the resistance of the child. Since the main purpose of this discussion is to understand *why* priests committed abuse rather than *how*, we will focus primarily on the first of Dr. Finkelhor's models.)

More than a quarter-century after it was proposed, this model continues to provide a coherent framework for considering why adults molest children, and for evaluating theories and research that have been published more recently. It provides the basis, for example, for a particularly succinct discussion of sexual abusers by Dr. Edward Rowan in his 2006 book, *Understanding Child Sexual Abuse*. This includes a wonderfully concise summary in non-technical language showing how the model can help to explain many different patterns of abusive behavior:

> There are common elements in these patterns even though the paths to the sexual abuse of children differ. The abuser first acknowledges children as sexual objects, either in their own right or as substitutes for adults, and then makes an emotional connection with the child to satisfy his own unmet needs. He typically lacks a meaningful adult sexual relationship and fails to develop a social conscience that says that sex with children is wrong, or an intervening variable causes previously good judgment to be temporarily or permanently suspended.

Much of this chapter will therefore be devoted to a discussion of the four factors that constitute the Finkelhor model, and how these factors may arise in the lives of individuals who become child molesters—and particularly in the lives of priests who do so. This discussion clearly owes a great deal to the work of the model's creator, and to its interpretation by Dr. Rowan. Other valuable sources include two reviews of the scientific literature concerning child sexual abuse compiled by Dr. Karen Terry and her colleagues at the John Jay College of Criminal Justice—one an adjunct to the College's 2004 *Nature and Scope* report, the other an integral part of a follow-up report that will be considered in a later chapter—and books by several authors devoted specifically to the topic of abuse by priests, who will be mentioned as their ideas are considered.

To be clear, this chapter will not attempt, as many of its sources did, to present a comprehensive review of current scientific thinking about abusive behavior; rather, it will use the template established by Dr. Finkelhor to present a selective survey of circumstances or experiences that could contribute to the development of such behavior, with a bias towards those most likely to be encountered by seminarians and priests. For the most part, the concepts included in the discussion enjoy as much empirical support as those that have been omitted; given that the ultimate goal is to understand why priests molested children, the bias in selecting these concepts seems justified.

As far as possible, these concepts are presented without using the technical jargon associated with them in the scientific literature. Ironically, the one technical term from this field that appears to be widely understood by the general public is in fact often misunderstood: the word "pedophile." Presumably because of its alliterative appeal, the phrase "pedophile priest" is popular with the media, but in many cases may not be strictly accurate. According to current diagnostic criteria, a pedophile is someone who experiences persistent and intense sexual attraction to prepubescent children, that is, to children who have not yet undergone puberty. Although the timing of puberty may differ considerably from one child to the next, since 1987 the generally accepted standard for the purpose of diagnosing pedophilia has been that "prepubescent" means aged 13 or under. But according to the *Nature and Scope* report, many victims of clerical abuse were older than this, making their abusers either "hebephiles" (if the victims were still in early puberty) or "ephebophiles" (if they were more mature). For these clerics, therefore, the term "pedophile priest" would not be technically correct.

That said, if pending revisions to the manual that defines psychiatric disorders are adopted, the diagnostic criteria for "pedophilic disorder" (as pedophilia would be renamed) will be expanded to include hebephilic behavior—in which case many more abusive priests would be eligible for the "pedophile" label. What matters most, of course, is not the label they are given but the fact that their behavior was and is completely abhorrent.

Having dealt with this important issue of nomenclature, we will now consider the four main factors in Dr. Finkelhor's model for abusive behavior by adults: sexual arousal, emotional congruence, blockage and disinhibition. (And for convenience, in the discussion that follows the word "pedophile" will be used in its soon-to-be-expanded sense.)

Sexual Arousal

As noted earlier, the ability of abusive males to become sexually aroused by children is one of the few aspects of their behavior that can be tested by prospective experiments. Typically, subjects are shown images of children and adults of both genders, and changes in blood flow to the penis are measured. In general, pedophiles do respond more than non-pedophiles to images of children. A 1998 review of multiple studies using this technique concluded that measurements of penile responses are the single most accurate way to predict which child molesters are most likely to re-offend.

This conclusion might, of course, be considered obvious; men would hardly be likely to pursue sexual relations that did not arouse them. Much less obvious is *why* these men experience arousal in response to children. No clear consensus appears on this point, presumably because there are multiple different answers to the question.   •

One theory in particular has garnered considerable attention, namely that molesters were themselves victims of sexual abuse at a young age. Their subsequent responsiveness to children is then seen either as a mechanism to exorcise the trauma of their own experience by repeating it with the roles reversed, or as a consequence of being conditioned by this experience to regard children as sex objects for adults.

When studies were first published indicating that many abusers had been victims as children, the significance of this finding was widely over-stated in the media, creating the impression that this single factor was all that was needed to explain abusive behavior. The reality is very different. Only a minority of molesters are former victims—a third or less, according to most studies—and only a small fraction of victims turn to abuse as adults. Moreover, very few women become child molesters, whereas many more girls than boys suffer sexual abuse. The only conclusion that can safely be drawn is that child molesters are more likely than non-molesters to have been victims of sexual abuse as children.

Non-abusive childhood sexual experiences, with peers rather than adults, have also been invoked to explain arousal in response to children. The theory goes that certain men enjoyed pleasurable encounters with other children when they were boys, which conditioned them to keep seeking pleasure from children even as they themselves grew older.

The pleasure of encounters with children is the basis for another hypothesis about misdirected sexual arousal, which holds that some men simply misinterpret the naturally affectionate response they feel towards children, or that children show towards them, so that it becomes a trigger for arousal.

Finally, biological factors—such as testosterone levels, chromosomal abnormalities or structural differences in the brain—have been proposed as explanations for adult arousal by children. In all cases, however, the proposals fail to explain why any increased sexual drive resulting from the biological condition would be directed specifically towards children.

Emotional Congruence

In important aspects of their personalities, child molesters are still children themselves, and relate more strongly to other children than to adults. This appears to be the main thrust of several theories offering to explain why molesters derive emotional gratification from their actions. Their interest in children as sex objects may be a permanent feature of their personalities, in which case it is said to be "fixated." Men in this category generally have little or no interest in adults as sexual partners, and are assumed to have undergone some sort of arrest in the normal process of psychosexual development. In that normal process, a juvenile's social and sexual interests are focused primarily on his own age group, and so evolve towards older individuals as he himself becomes older; in a fixated pedophile, the argument goes, this process was interrupted, and his interests remain frozen at whatever point his development stalled.

Many molesters, however, are considered to be "regressed" rather than fixated: they did progress through the normal stages of psychosexual development and are primarily interested in adults, but may "regress" under severe stress to more childlike psychological and sexual interests. Typically, they then select female victims and feel guilt and remorse for their actions—in contrast to fixated pedophiles, who are more likely to select male victims and to show little regret for abusing them.

The brake that halts the psychosexual development of a fixated pedophile is believed to be either emotional trauma or emotional deprivation. In the first case, the trauma might result from sexual abuse—whose potential also to induce sexual responsiveness to children was noted above—or from abuse in some other form, either emotional or physical. In the second case, when development is arrested by emotional deprivation rather than trauma, the affected adult is supposedly searching for the emotional fulfillment he was denied as a youngster, which he does by looking for a child in his own image to whom he can give the love he never had.

Not all theories in this category hark back to childhood experiences of the abuser. Several others center on the sense of power and control that an abuser may derive from his interactions with children, which he may lack in his relationships with adults because of low self-esteem, and/or may be encouraged to pursue by the stereotypes he has absorbed of dominant behavior by adult males.

As an aside, these ideas illustrate that the distinctions between the four factors in the Finkelhor model are not always sharp, and that some potential triggers of abuse appear to correspond to more than one factor. The abuser's feeling of power and control could be classified as contributing to both emotional congruence and disinhibition, while the unsatisfactory adult relationships that help to enhance this feeling might be regarded as a form of blockage.

Similarly, the distinction between fixated and regressed pedophiles is nowadays regarded as less absolute than it was when this classification was first proposed in the late 1970s; these categories are now seen as the extremes of a continuum, with many men falling in between. Presumably, the same factors that cause the arrest of psychosexual development in fixated pedophiles are also responsible for the tendency of regressed pedophiles to revert to immature sexual interests, but have a lesser impact on these individuals.

Blockage

The ease with which many abusers relate to children stands in sharp contrast to the difficulty they often experience with adults, which typically limits or blocks their ability to form sexual relationships with age-appropriate peers.

This is particularly true when those peers are female; many child molesters really struggle to relate to women. The Freudian view is that these men are displaying unresolved Oedipal conflicts concerning their mothers. More testable theories are that their first sexual encounters with women were so traumatic— for example, because of impotence or humiliating rejection—that they are deterred from trying again; or that they have suffered the recent loss or disruption of a relationship. In the latter case the molester's interest in children may be temporary, the result of regression under stress as described in the previous section.

Illustrating again that certain issues appear to be correspond to more than one of the four factors in the model, arrested psychosexual development—noted above as a cause of emotional congruence—can also be considered a cause of blockage, because it leads to a lack of interest in sex with adults.

The obstacle that stands in the way of healthy relationships may not always be specifically sexual. There is good evidence that many child abusers are lonely and introverted, with poor social skills, all of which hinders their ability to form intimate connections with other adults. These difficulties may reflect lingering insecurities caused by a failure to form close attachments to parents at a young age.

Another non-sexual barrier that may prevent abusers from forming close relationships is narcissism—which in clinical parlance means rather more than the excessive self-admiration it usually denotes in everyday conversation. To a psychologist, a narcissist is someone who is unduly preoccupied with himself, has a strong sense of entitlement, believes that he deserves special treatment, and lacks empathy for others. Superficially, narcissists can make excellent company, but at a deeper level they are often highly insecure, and hampered in intimate relationships by their excessive focus on their own needs.

After two theories that rely on non-sexual issues to explain abusers' difficulties with adult relationships, one final hypothesis puts sex back in the spotlight. This holds that the molester's own repressive attitudes towards sex prevent him from pursuing carnal relations with other adults. The obvious gap in this hypothesis is that it fails to explain why sexual contact with a child would be less objectionable.

Disinhibition

Even with all of the other three factors in place, a man on the verge of making sexual advances to a child still has to take the fateful decision to break society's strict taboos against this behavior. A variety of factors may contribute to his ultimate willingness to do so: narcissism (again), alcohol use, "self talk," impulsivity, stress, childhood conditioning, and cultural norms.

Narcissism, which we have just considered as a cause of blockage, is another of those issues that ticks more than one box in the four-factor checklist, since the personality characteristics that define it are directly relevant to the process of disinhibition. A narcissist who is feeling attracted to and aroused by a child might easily conclude that he is entitled to gratify himself by engaging in sexual activity with the youngster, and would have little concern about the impact of this activity on his victim.

Alcohol does of course cause a loss of inhibition in many aspects of behavior, so it is hardly surprising that the evidence linking alcohol use to sexual abuse is some of the strongest in this whole field of research. Multiple studies have shown that a significant percentage of child molesters are alcoholics and/or were drinking at the time they committed abuse. Estimates of this percentage differ from one report to another, but 30-40 percent seems typical, with somewhat higher figures in several studies.

"Self talk," as the phrase implies, is a process by which abusers talk themselves into believing that their actions are acceptable. They may persuade themselves, for example, that their behavior is not really causing harm; that they are not responsible because the victim led them on; that parents are at fault for allowing access to the victim; and so on. Most molesters rely on a concoction of such excuses and justifications—"cognitive distortions" in the language of psychiatrists—to deflect any sense of shame or guilt, allowing them both to initiate and to repeat acts that should otherwise be taboo.

The evidence that poor impulse control plays an important role in overcoming taboos against child abuse is less clear. Indeed, fixated molesters are often the opposite of impulsive, "grooming" their victims over a period of time, and building up gradually to the eventual initiation of abuse. In those cases where impulsivity is a factor, the molester is much more likely to fall into the regressed category—someone whose usual preference is for adult partners but who may turn to a child under duress.

Stress, too, is more likely to be a disinhibiting factor for regressed than for fixated offenders. Loneliness, the loss of a job, the break-up of a relationship: all have been suggested as stressors that could tip a regressed offender over the edge into an abusive act.

Another theory holds that conditioning from youthful sexual experiences with other children helps to reduce inhibitions about seeking similar experiences as an adult. Children often engage in various forms of sexual play that go unpunished even if detected; as a result, some participants may be conditioned to regard such interactions as acceptable, even later on in life when they are significantly older than their "playmates."

The perception that abusive behavior will be tolerated forms the basis of the final theories worth noting about disinhibition. These maintain that men are encouraged by many cultural norms to behave as they wish, in sexual as well as other matters. Faced with an opportunity for sexual gratification, the abuser may feel that it his right to seize that opportunity—or at the very least, that he will not be condemned for doing so.

CLERICAL OFFENDERS

How, then, do these four factors apply in the case of abusive priests? What specific experiences might have caused them to become abusive? And to what extent did their training contribute to their behavior?

To place these questions in the right context, we should note that the experiences we are seeking to identify would not necessarily have been encountered by all future priests, or even a majority; while the outrage over their behavior has justifiably been huge, abusive priests actually represent a fairly small percentage of the overall clerical population. To be clear, this percentage should be zero; no child should ever be abused by an adult, let alone by a priest. That said, the overall figure reported by the *Nature and Scope* report for the population of priests in service between 1950 and 2002 was a modest four percent (although for priests ordained during the 1960s and early 1970s, the percentage was more than twice that figure). By way of comparison, according to a 2002 article by Dr. Thomas Plante, one of the leading experts in the field, the corresponding figure is between two and five percent for clergymen in other religious traditions, and about eight percent for the male population as a whole. While no comfort can be drawn from the implication that priests were no worse than other men—they should of course be much better—these figures do suggest that priests were no more likely than other men to experience and respond to the four factors that lead to abusive behavior.

Clearly, though, many priests did experience these factors. Certain common features in their backgrounds may help to explain how they did so. The four factors in the Finkelhor model effectively represent the intersection between an individual's personal history and his current circumstances—and with respect to these intersecting issues, clerical abusers form a much more homogeneous group than abusers in the wider population. Depending on their point of entry into seminary training, most followed one of two general paths to become priests: either they enrolled in a minor seminary as a young adolescent when their psychosexual development was still at a relatively early stage, or they began their training in a major seminary after they had already reached adulthood. Most then spent a further period of up to eight years in preparation for ordination, were assigned to parishes with similar responsibilities and living conditions, and waited a number of years (typically about ten, according to data in the *Nature and Scope* report) before committing their first act of abuse.

In the context of the four-factor model of abusive behavior, the different points of entry into seminary training are highly significant. The main triggers that can lead to sexual responsiveness to children, or to emotional congruence with them, have that impact only if they occur early in the person's psychosexual development. The same is also true of a subset of the triggers that lead to blockage and disinhibition. Only in the case of priests who began their training as boys, therefore, could the seminary system have been responsible for exposing future abusers to these triggers. Men who began their training as adults must have been exposed to them elsewhere; the environment inside major seminaries may then have reinforced any damage done by earlier experiences, but the initial damage would have been inflicted outside the seminary system.

§

These points duly noted, we can now consider how the four-factor model applies in the case of abusive priests, starting with those who did attend minor seminaries. To judge from my own experience at Upholland, as described in previous chapters, these priests would have been exposed to multiple circumstances that could—according to the model—have predisposed them to abusive behavior.

They might, for example, have been sexually abused by an older boy (as I almost was) or have engaged in consensual sexual acts with other boys (a strong enough possibility that rules were in place to prevent it); either occurrence could have left them with the capacity to be sexually aroused by children.

Almost certainly, they would have experienced some degree of emotional trauma because of the loneliness induced by extreme isolation from their families. In my own case, as we saw, this loneliness was severe enough to induce a protracted episode of highly disturbed behavior, my phony appendicitis. In the case of future abusers, the impact may have been even more severe, arresting their psychosexual development and leaving them with a permanent preference for the company of children of similar age to their own at the time of the arrest.

Even for those who did not suffer severe psychological trauma, the isolation of seminary life would have hampered emotional maturation. With no opportunity to interact with their secular peers, girls as well as boys, minor seminarians were deprived of emotional experiences that are an important part of growing up. Instead, they were subjected to the "closed culture" that so bothered the National Review Board in its 2004 report on the abuse crisis.

The nature and impact of this culture are described with great eloquence by Raymond Hedin in his account of life in the Milwaukee minor seminary, *Married to the Church*:

> Our sole duties were to study, pray, and keep the rules—and thus, by these self-oriented, asocial activities, become holy. We were so protected that many of us barely experienced adolescence at all—at the time. One classmate, now a therapist, is fond of saying that he entered the seminary in 1957 at age thirteen and left eight years later at age thirteen. His story is more the rule than the exception....
>   ...We were expected to enter the seminary as boys and to come out twelve years later as priests; no one thought much about the need to become men along the way... The ideas that learning was active, that certain developmental struggles might be necessary to maturation, that "priesthood" was not a state to be conferred by ceremony but the culmination of considerable intellectual, psychological, and emotional processes, did not register.
>   The seminary did everything it could to ignore emotions in the seeming hope that these messy forces would simply go away...
>   By extension, sexuality was an unfortunate encumbrance, an ineradicable problem that could never be licked, so to speak, but could be held in check through the help of grace, a kind of spiritual steroid always available to help us transcend our natural limits.

The consequences of this culture were apparent in a study of 217 active American priests conducted at the start of the 1970s by Dr. Eugene Kennedy, a psychologist at Loyola University. By his assessment, a mere 6 percent of these priests were psychologically and emotionally developed; the remainder he classified as either still developing (29 percent), underdeveloped (57 percent), or "maldeveloped" (8 percent). The priests whose development was incomplete— the great majority—were more comfortable with teenagers and had few friends their own age: signs both of emotional congruence with children and blockage from relationships with adults. Tellingly, the area in which these priests were most underdeveloped was in their psychosexual maturity. They had not yet learned how to deal with their sexual feelings, and therefore invested an inordinate amount of energy in dealing with them, and found intimate friendships difficult because of their uncertainty over these feelings. Although there is no record to indicate what percentage of these priests began their training in minor seminaries, the fact that so many were psychosexually immature suggests that it was significant. So too do the findings of a contemporaneous study of six thousand priests by the National Opinion Research Center (NORC), which reported that three-fifths of American clergy graduated from high school before entering a seminary—suggesting that the other two-fifths must have attended minor seminaries.

One of the key individuals who conducted the NORC study, it should be noted, has been highly critical of Kennedy's findings about the emotional maturity of priests. The individual in question is one of the most prominent members of the clergy in the US, Professor/Doctor/Father Andrew Greeley, a sociologist and novelist as well as a priest. Greeley's main concern is that Kennedy's study did not include a matched group of men who were not priests, so there is no way of knowing whether his assessment methods would have produced a similar result for adult males in general. As evidence that it might have done, Greeley cites a personality test administered to a quarter of the priests in the NORC study whose results *were* compared with those for other groups, and showed that priests were just as "self-actualized" as other American males of the same age, with no evidence of any greater deficiency in their capacity to form intimate friendships.

While Greeley's criticism of Kennedy's methodology is fair, the implication that the NORC data disprove Kennedy's conclusions may not be. The self-actualization test administered by NORC was designed to measure the respondent's degree of dependence on others, and the extent to which "he is guided by internal motivations rather than external influences." While undoubtedly relevant to a priest's behavior, these attributes would not necessarily correlate, in my view, with his psychosexual maturity; a priest could be quite satisfied and "inner-directed" (to use the language of self-actualization psychology) in many other aspects of his life, but still be emotionally immature with respect to relationships. Indeed, too much self-satisfaction and inner-direction might conceivably translate into narcissism and self-talk, and thus into disinhibition of abusive behavior.

Also worth noting is that if priests were in fact just like other American males of the same age with respect to "intimacy skills," some small percentage of them would have been child molesters anyway; as we saw earlier, although evidence on the subject is scanty, the percentage of adult males who molest children appears to be slightly higher than the percentage of priests identified as abusers in the *Nature and Scope* report.

Drawing on my own personal experience to comment on Kennedy's work, I find his observation about priests spending an inordinate amount of energy dealing with their sexual feelings highly credible; it reminds me strongly of my own difficulties when puberty arrived, which as we saw in the previous chapter, were a major factor in the stress that led to my feigning appendicitis. The challenge with sexual feelings was that they were pleasurable, irrepressible and morally ruinous all at the same time. My biological self would have liked nothing more than to give in to them, but to do so would jeopardize both my vocation and my eternal salvation. And on those occasions when I did lapse, any pleasure I derived was immediately overwhelmed by much stronger feelings of guilt and shame—whose impact was only reinforced by the constant realization that celibacy was a defining requirement of the priesthood I was pursuing. As a result, a good part of my mental energy went into intercepting and suppressing sexual thoughts before they could trigger any further damage to my clerical ambition and immortal soul.

Because these issues were so fundamental, I assume that other seminarians went through essentially the same mental processes as I did (although such was the taboo around sexual matters at Upholland, my classmates and I would never have dreamed of comparing notes on the subject). I can also imagine that the never-ending cycle of temptation, struggle, occasional lapse and deep guilt continued indefinitely for those who became priests—particularly since, as we will shortly see, there is good evidence that very few of them succeeded in completely renouncing sexual activity after ordination.

The shame experienced by future priests when they failed to control their sexual urges is central to another hypothesis about abusive clerical behavior. In an article he contributed to *The Sex Offender*, a book published in 2002, D.R Hands argues that "shame cycles" induced by failure to meet unrealistic moral expectations stunted the psychosexual development of certain priests, causing them to ignore rather than deal with their sexual feelings; not to be denied, these feelings then broke through years later as an obsession.

Fr. Donald Cozzens, a former seminary rector and a wise commentator on many aspects of the Church and the priesthood, expressed similar concerns in his book *Sacred Silence: Denial and the Crisis in the Church*, which he was completing just as the 2002 abuse scandals were unfolding in Boston:

> A system... suspicious of the fundamental value and goodness of human sexuality demands exceptional and psychosexual maturity of its candidates for the priesthood. Without such unusual qualities of personality and character, seminarians are likely to make attempts to ignore their sexual energies and interests; in other words, repress them. Eventually, repression rebels. Renouncing a sexual life and at the same time often preoccupied with sex, a seminarian is likely to be disposed during his seminary years or well into his priesthood to unhealthy and even profoundly destructive expressions of sexuality.

This view is clearly consistent with Eugene Kennedy's findings, and with the concept noted earlier that repressive sexual attitudes can contribute to an abuser's behavior. In that earlier note these attitudes were classified as contributing to blockage of adult relationships rather than to emotional congruence with children—which is how they might be classified if their impact really is to arrest psychosexual development. Such ambiguity with respect to their appropriate classification is of course much less important than the likelihood that these attitudes played a significant role in abusive behavior by priests.

Indeed, there may be yet another way in which they contributed to such behavior: by encouraging habits of "self talk," a behavior that would be classified in the four-factor model as disinhibition. My basis for this conclusion is the way that I myself dealt with "sins of impurity" when the time came for Confession, as it usually did every week. Under Catholic doctrine, a sin can only be "mortal"—one that would consign the sinner to hell if not confessed and forgiven—if it is committed deliberately and with full knowledge. A salacious thought is not by itself a mortal sin, but becomes one if the thinker consciously decides to entertain it. For me (and presumably other boys), the difficulty this created was the constant need to be auditing my thought processes and classifying them as deliberate or not. Did I stop thinking about that girl's body quickly enough, the moment I realized what I was doing? Or did I let the thought linger too long? When I woke up with an erection last night, did I do my best to ignore it until it faded away? Or did I take pleasure from the sensation, even for a moment? These were very real concerns that bothered me almost every day, and particularly as I prepared my list of sins for Confession each week. Anxious to avoid a list that was embarrassingly long, I probably self-talked my way out of many sins that really met the criteria, persuading myself that my intent had not been clear or my awareness complete. In other words, I rationalized and justified to myself behavior that I should have considered sinful. Conceivably, abusive priests who developed the same sort of thought processes in the seminary then adapted these processes to rationalize their abusive behavior to themselves.

Seminary life may also have encouraged one other potentially dangerous way of thinking: narcissism. In this case the conclusion is based not so much on my own experience—although my primary interest in the priesthood was, as we saw in Chapter 1, a childish wish to be the center of attention—but on reflections offered by Raymond Hedin in *Married to the Church*, his account of life in the Milwaukee minor seminary. Having introduced the idea that this institution "offered the balm of seminarian specialness," he goes on to explain that:

> Specialness, however, was also, in psychological and social terms, the atmosphere we already walked in, a sense of ourselves we were given without any effort on our part. By simple virtue of entering the seminary we became kings in our home parishes, princes in our own families. When I returned home for vacations, my grade-school nuns would gather around after mass, laughing at my stories; my parents' friends would congratulate me on my presumed good work. At Christmas and Easter, all the seminarians would march down the aisle before mass, the valiant troops home on leave. In the words of one classmate, we felt "totally reinforced from the outside," and the reinforcement worked its way in.

> In that sense, in our otherwise relatively ascetic context, specialness was
> our licensed narcotic, our prescribed intoxicant... the seminarian of our day
> was special by anticipation as well as acclamation. Within the Catholic
> community, we shared the priest's cultic status...

Reinforced over the years, the sense of entitlement that often accompanies
such a strong sense of specialness could have played a significant role in the
willingness of priests to override the constraints that normally prevent abusive
behavior.

§

At the age of eighteen, those minor seminarians who still aspired to the
priesthood typically moved straight on to a major seminary, where they were
joined by other young adults who had decided more recently to pursue the same
aspiration. From this point forward the paths of early and late recruits merged,
so that they were all exposed to essentially the same environment. In a moment,
we will consider what pro-abusive triggers they may have encountered together.
First, however, we should ask how the incoming young adults might have
encountered those triggers that are believed to act primarily during earlier stages
of development, and to which younger recruits had been exposed in minor
seminary.

For the most part, the answer probably lies in their being members of strict
Catholic families that were just as repressive about sexual matters as minor
seminaries were, and just as discouraging about relationships with the opposite
sex. In my own family, certainly, sex was a completely taboo subject. Despite
my mother's frequent pregnancies, we never discussed how babies were made.
And while dating was obviously never an option for me, my mother made it
extremely difficult for my siblings too. The first of my brothers to have a
girlfriend had a major fight with my parents over the issue; the oldest of my
sisters got into enormous trouble because a busybody in the neighborhood saw
her holding hands with a boy after school and told my mother. The majority of
Catholic families were not, I suspect, quite as strict—but nor did they produce
sons who wanted to be priests. Those that did were probably just as rigid as
mine, so that their teenage sons went through agonies of conscience over
sexuality similar to those experienced by minor seminarians, with similar
consequences. And even though they had not been subjected as adolescents to
the extreme isolation of seminary life, when it came to developing social skills
with girls they might just as well have been.

Some percentage of the adult entrants to major seminaries might also have
been victims of abuse in their younger years, or have had other traumatic
experiences that predisposed them to abusive behavior.

One other real possibility is that, consciously or not, young men who
enrolled in major seminaries were attempting to escape from sexual difficulties
of which they were already aware. If sex was going to be a major problem, why
not simply eliminate it? During the highly intolerant period when most abusers

were trained, this line of thought might have been particularly appealing to men who had realized they were homosexual—an orientation that is still frowned on by the Church today, and which decades ago was almost unmentionable. Any extra appeal the priesthood held for gay men might help to explain another of the key statistics noted in the *Nature and Scope* report, that over eighty percent of all abuse victims were male. While there is no evidence that gay men are any more likely than others to molest children, the presence of a higher proportion of such men in the priesthood would be expected on a purely statistical basis to have increased the percentage of victims who were male. (In this context, it is also worth noting that during the late 1960s and early 1970s a large number of presumably heterosexual priests resigned to get married, a development that would have further increased the proportion of gay men in the priesthood.)

§

Whatever psychological baggage they had accumulated by this stage of their lives, the new adult recruits and former minor seminarians were not about to be relieved of it by their experiences in major seminaries. These institutions were just as isolated and sexually repressive as their minor counterparts, and offered no opportunity to erase any lingering damage from prior sexual experiences, to catch up on delayed psychosexual maturation, or to improve interpersonal skills with secular peers. Nor would they have done much to reverse any sense of specialness and entitlement that incoming students may have harbored; on the contrary, their glorification of all things ecclesiastical might have encouraged new recruits to develop what might be called "institutional narcissism," a sense that the Church and its actions were extraordinarily special.

In due course, men who made it through the eight arduous years of major seminary (or six in England) were ordained. At which point their lives were immediately transformed—not just by their newly elevated status, but by an abrupt change in their circumstances. For many years they had lived in tightly knit communities, surrounded by like-minded peers whom they had known for most of their adult lives, and in some cases since adolescence. Now they found themselves consigned to unfamiliar suburban parishes, isolated from their friends, living with pastors who were usually much older and often curmudgeonly. For many priests (and especially those ordained in the 1950s and 1960s, as will be explained in Chapter 8), this was the first time they fully grasped the magnitude of the sacrifices to which they had committed. As time went by they became increasingly lonely, but often found it hard to make friends in their new communities, their status as priests too great an obstacle for their awkward social skills to surmount. In the NORC survey of American clergy in 1970, loneliness was the third most frequently mentioned "great problem" experienced by priests, cited by 16 percent (about one sixth) of respondents. Although this was smaller than the percentage who cited the way authority is used in the Church (29 percent) or the difficulty of getting through to people

(17 percent), loneliness was the strongest predictor of resignations from the priesthood, most of which were precipitated by the desire to marry.

Implicit in this last finding is that loneliness accentuated the burden of celibacy, making the daily battle to suppress carnal longings a constant reminder of the priest's vow to forgo the closest of all human relationships. Surprisingly, though, only 12 percent of priests in the NORC survey cited celibacy as a major problem; even among younger priests—those under 35—the figure was only 18 percent, placing it fifth on their list of major grouses.

While these figures imply that most priests do not find celibacy too much of a struggle, the research of Dr. Richard Sipe strongly suggests otherwise. Sipe, a psychologist and former priest, has spent several decades studying the practice of celibacy by the Catholic clergy, interviewing about a thousand priests in the process. On the evidence of this substantial body of work, he concludes that only a small percentage of priests remain completely celibate, and that at any one time, about half are engaged in various patterns of sexual activity with other people. When Sipe first published his findings in 1990 in the book *Celibacy in Crisis* they caused a firestorm, attracting criticism of his methodology from Andrew Greeley and of his conclusions from many others. But while his statistical methods may indeed be open to question, they did produce a reasonably accurate estimate of the percentage of priests engaged in sexual activity with minors: Sipe's figure of six percent falls between the figures of four percent and eight percent reported in the *Nature and Scope* report for, respectively, all priests in service between 1950 and 2002, and those ordained in the 1960s and early 1970s.

And so we arrive at the culmination of the process we have been describing, the one by which priests became abusers. Predisposed by childhood experiences (in some cases within seminaries) to relate sexually and emotionally to children, lonely because of their situations and inadequate social skills (another legacy of seminary life), unable any longer to control their sexual urges, a small percentage of priests chose to gratify these urges by molesting children. The trust that they enjoyed from both children and families gave them relatively easy access to potential victims, as did their daily contact with altar boys. Whatever inhibitions they had about making advances to children were overcome by their loneliness and frustration, and often by the consumption of alcohol. Also contributing to the "disinhibition" process was the clerical culture within the Church, which (according to Richard Sipe and another well-informed commentator, the psychiatrist Dr. Len Sperry) promoted a sense of entitlement and of dominion over other people—particularly (in Sipe's view) with respect to sexual matters. And time after time, some poor child became another victim.

Then came the aftermath: the psychological and spiritual harm to the victim that barely registered with the abuser; the latter's rationalization and justification of his actions to himself, drawing on the habit of self-talk he had learned over many years of preparing for Confession.

Only rarely did the aftermath include an early complaint by the victim to Church authorities; most victims kept what had happened to themselves, and did not report it until years or decades later. But in cases when they did complain more quickly, the response was usually unsympathetic, if not hostile. Many were fobbed off with promises that the Church would take care of Father's problem, and/or offered settlements that were conditional upon them keeping the abuse a secret. Molesters, in the meantime, were often sent away for courses of ineffective treatment and then reassigned to new parishes, with no disclosure of their abusive histories, and so no limits on their access to children. And in too many instances, predictably, the outcome was yet further abuse—abuse that could and should have been prevented by the Church, but was not.

§

Thus did priests become abusers. For most who did this was a slow process; according to the *Nature and Scope* report, as noted earlier, the average lapse of time between ordination and first offence was about ten years—which means that the typical abuser did not commit his first offence until about twenty years after entering a seminary, an important point we will return to later. Just over half of the priests who did commit abuse stopped after their first victim, and may therefore belong to a group characterized by Richard Sipe as belatedly passing through a developmental phase they had been denied during adolescence. The remaining offenders had multiple victims, in some cases dozens, suggesting an inability ever to move beyond that development phase, and/or a stronger compulsion to molest children.

While the foregoing discussion may explain why priests became abusers, it does not explain why they did so in increasing numbers between 1950 and 1980, nor why abuse then declined so rapidly. Understanding these changes in the behavior of priests is clearly crucial to avoiding any repetition of the abuse epidemic, and will therefore be the main focus of the final chapter. First, though, we will return to Upholland to learn about the impact of the Second Vatican Council on seminary life—a topic that will prove highly relevant to understanding the timing and course of the epidemic.

CHAPTER 7

CHANGING TIMES:
UPHOLLAND COLLEGE, 1965-69

In the autumn of 1965, while my classmates and I were adjusting to life in the Higher Line, one of the most momentous events in the history of the Catholic Church was reaching its climax. For the fourth consecutive autumn the Second Vatican Council convened in Rome, this time for what would be its final sessions. Thus far the Council's impact at Upholland had been confined mainly to the chapel, where English had replaced Latin for all but the central "Canon" of our daily Low Mass. But in October 1965, a document emerged that over the next few years would lead to radical changes in seminary life: *Optatam Totius,* the Council's decree on priestly formation. Although it took care to reiterate the historical precepts of the Council of Trent, the decree also included a number of modernizing concepts, including the following statement about an appropriate way of life for minor seminarians:

> Their daily routine should be in accord with the age, the character and the stage of development of adolescence and fully adapted to the norms of a healthy psychology. Nor should the fitting opportunity be lacking for social and cultural contacts and for contact with one's own family.

In some respects, what this said about the operation of seminaries was not very different from the exhortations of Pius XII in 1950, which—as we saw in Chapter 4—did little to change these institutions. Fifteen years later, however, the inclination to change was much greater both in society and within the Church, and this time the recommendations did result in action.

Locally in Liverpool, the Archbishop responded by asking Upholland's Board of Governors to review the disciplinary code and recommend changes. None of this, it should be said, was apparent to us in the minor seminary— neither the issuance of *Optatam Totius* nor the Archbishop's response; even in matters directly affecting the Church and the future of seminary training, we were still very much isolated from the outside world. The Board's recommendations were therefore a complete (but highly pleasant) surprise to us when they were announced in May 1966, near the end of our first year in the Higher Line. The two most immediate were particularly welcome. As of the next academic year, we would enjoy a three-day break at home in the middle of each term. Just as welcome, we would be allowed to bring bicycles back to the seminary and, with advance permission, to leave the College grounds by ourselves on unsupervised rides.

For me in particular, the second of these innovations provided rather more freedom than the College authorities had intended. Their expectation was that bikes would be used just for local excursions, but as an enthusiastic summertime cyclist I was fit enough to venture much further afield. My trusty two-wheeler had come back with me when I returned to Upholland that September, and after several long jaunts in the local area I hatched an ambitious plan to sneak home for a brief visit. By my calculation, if I left immediately after lunch on a "sports afternoon" I would have enough time to ride the fifteen miles home, spend about forty-five minutes there, and be back in time for tea at a quarter to five. All without the College authorities knowing.

On October 18, 1966, a Tuesday, I had the first opportunity to test my scheme. Having obtained permission to go for a ride that afternoon I bolted down my lunch, jumped on my bike, and pedaled furiously for over an hour to reach home. As I parked my bike outside the back door I was feeling mightily pleased with myself; everything was going to plan. That all changed a moment later when I opened the door and found my aunt rather than my mother in the kitchen. Where, I asked her, was Mum? "In the hospital," she replied, "with your new baby sister."

I was dumbstruck. Implausible though it may seem—given that I was almost sixteen and had just spent most of the summer at home—I had not realized that my mother was pregnant. My failure to do so was the result of both ignorance and gullibility: ignorance about all aspects of human reproduction, and gullibility in believing the story my parents had concocted to explain my mother's swollen midriff. Earlier in the summer she had spent some time in hospital, and when she returned home my father had told us that her stomach was heavily bandaged following an operation. The fallacy of this story might have become apparent if we had seen her again around the house, but she hid herself away in her bedroom under the pretence of recuperating from surgery. Had I known more about the "facts of life" I might never have swallowed the initial story, but since I didn't, the idea that my mother might be pregnant never once occurred to me. Hence my astonishment when my aunt told me the news.

My parents' efforts to conceal my mother's condition were, I assume, the result of sheer embarrassment. By this time my mother was forty-eight years old, and must have been mortified to find herself pregnant again—particularly in a household where sex was a taboo subject and four of her children were now teenagers. Her response was to stay out of sight, from us and indeed everyone else. This established a pattern she found difficult to break; for many years afterwards she was an almost total recluse, hardly ever leaving the house.

During my ride back to Upholland I had plenty to feel embarrassed about myself, as I tried to understand how I could possibly have been so ignorant and naïve about my mother's condition. I had last seen her only five weeks earlier; how could I not have realized that she was pregnant?

Fortunately I did not have to say anything to anyone when I got back to the seminary. Officially I did not know that I had a new sister, and for the moment I was happy to keep it that way. A few days later my father did call the College with the news, which was duly relayed to me. By then I had adjusted to the idea, and could avoid showing the surprise my aunt must have seen when she first told me about the newborn.

§

Four weeks later I was home again, this time with no need for secrecy, as we enjoyed our first-ever mid-term break. My new sister was of course the center of attention. Having forgotten what my youngest brother had looked like six years earlier, I found it hard to believe that a human being could be so small. Had I known more about reproductive biology at the time, I would also have been grateful that she was born with all of her wits, limbs and organs intact; given my mother's unusually advanced age the chance of birth defects must have been high, but my sister escaped them.

As anticipated, the mid-term break made the long first term much more tolerable. By the time we returned after the break, Christmas was less than six weeks away. Admittedly, the weeks in question were the gloomiest of the year, with the sun going down by four in the afternoon—ruling out any further trips home on the bike. But compared with the long periods of isolation we knew so well, six weeks seemed like nothing. In no time at all it was Boxing Day, and we were on our way home once again.

§

Lent is a time for soul-searching and penance, and my Lenten deliberations that year led me inexorably to a life-changing decision: to abandon my quest for the priesthood. After two years of fighting to preserve my "vocation" against daily assaults from "impure thoughts," I realized that I did not want to spend the rest of my life in a continual struggle to remain chaste; it was already clear to me that the effort would be doomed to failure. Celibacy, which had seemed inconsequential when I first signed up for the seminary at the age of eleven, now seemed utterly impossible. The flimsiness of my motivation to become a priest—my wish to be the center of attention in a packed church every Sunday—

was no match for the primeval urges that ensure the continuation of the human race.

By coincidence, Hollywood provided me with the perfect quotation to summarize my new resolve. *A Man for All Seasons* had been released just a few months earlier, and at one point its hero, St. Thomas More, was asked why he decided against becoming a clergyman. "Because I would rather be a good husband than a bad priest," he replied. My sentiments exactly.

In reaching my decision at that particular juncture, I was also influenced by the convenience of its timing. In a few months' time I would be taking my O-level exams, which represented a natural breakpoint in my education. Come what may, I would be transitioning in September to a new course of study for A-levels, and could do that just as easily at another school. My two older brothers had both attended St. Edward's College in Liverpool, and I assumed I would be able to transfer there.

The challenge now was to tell my parents. This was going to be difficult. Tempted as I was to inform them by letter, I realized that I needed to do so in person. One step at a time, though; I would start with my father. A few days into the Easter vacation I managed to corner him alone in the sitting room. Forging ahead before I lost my nerve, I blurted out that I wanted to leave Upholland at the end of the summer term and transfer to St. Edward's.

My father's usual reaction to unexpected news was to sit quietly and digest it, which is exactly what he did in response to my outburst. He then asked me how long I had been thinking of leaving, and how sure I was about doing so. After reflecting on my answers—"months" and "very"—he quietly offered me two reasons to reconsider my decision. First, he said, my disillusionment with the priesthood might just be a temporary phase, which would pass if I gave myself more time. While I was pretty sure that this would not be the case, there was absolutely no way I could discuss my reasons for thinking so with my father. We could no more have engaged in a conversation related to sex than we could have flown an Apollo spacecraft to the Moon. My father's second objection was that my education would be significantly disrupted if I were to shift schools at this relatively late stage; if I could tolerate life at Upholland for two more years I should stay there until I had completed my A-levels. This argument carried more weight with me, although not really enough by itself to dissuade me from leaving.

There was a third issue to consider, however, much bigger than those my father had raised, that hovered over our discussion without either of us addressing it directly: the explosion we could expect from my mother. I had no need to ask my father how she would react. My childhood experience had taught me only too well how she could explode with little provocation, and in this case she had a huge amount of emotion invested in the idea of my becoming a priest. To her it would be immaterial that I, not she, would have to commit to a life of hard sacrifice; her life's dream was to have a son in the priesthood, and my obligation was to make this come true. The merest suggestion that I might not do so would trigger a massive eruption, followed by a battle royal with her over my future.

At some point I would have no choice but to engage in that battle, but after thinking things over I decided to defer it for the moment. Two more years at Upholland seemed a less daunting prospect than life at home in the aftermath of civil war with my mother. So a few days later I told my father I would stay on for my A-levels, and review the decision again once these were completed.

§

Ordination Day 1967 fell on May 20, and was notable for two innovations. The first was a new venue, and a magnificent one at that. Liverpool's new Metropolitan Cathedral had been consecrated only six days earlier, and now became the site of the ordination ceremony that had always been held at Upholland. The second innovation followed logically from the first. Since we had all been bussed into Liverpool for the ceremony, we went directly to our own homes afterwards to begin the mid-term break.

That first ordination ceremony in the new cathedral was the most memorable of the fourteen I attended. By the time we arrived in Liverpool we were all in a boisterous mood, excited about seeing the new cathedral and about the three days at home that would follow. From the moment we entered the building, however, we were awed into silence by its majesty. The design of the cathedral may be controversial to this day, but the visual impact of its cavernous vaulted space and kaleidoscopic interior light is genuinely stunning. In this new setting the ordination ceremony seemed transformed, even more full of pomp and solemnity than before. At no point was this more evident than during the prostration, with the ordinands stretched out in long white albs on the floor of the sanctuary, dwarfed by their surroundings, bathed in colored light cascading down from the huge stained-glass crown high above. Truly a striking image!

§

The weeks after Ordination Day were a blur of study, memorization and stress as I prepared for and sat my nine O-level exams. The results were not due to appear until the start of September, so I tried to put them out of my mind while I spent an enjoyable summer working in my first paid job. For the princely sum of £6 a week I was employed in the quality-control lab at my father's company, checking the thickness of the gold layer on electroplated computer parts. The work involved intriguing manipulations with hydraulic presses, resin blocks and microscopes, making me feel very technical, and reinforcing my fascination with science. More intriguing still was the pretty girl in the front office, who seemed to enjoy teasing the boss's seminarian son to see just how easily she could draw a blush. As the summer wore on my interest in becoming a celibate clergyman declined even further; a married scientist was what I wanted to be.

For the moment, however, this change of direction would have to wait. I had committed to serve out another two years at Upholland, so when September came I headed dutifully back to the seminary. At least I had good news to cheer me on my way. The O-level results had arrived just a few days earlier, and I had passed all nine subjects. In my new quest for a career in science, these results were a good first step towards securing a place at university.

§

The enjoyment I derived from my studies helped to offset my lingering dissatisfaction at being back in the seminary, and at the uncertainty over my eventual exit. And then, thanks to an unexpected development, these studies also became a clear path to that exit. In keeping with other steps they had taken to reduce our isolation from the outside world, the College authorities decided that junior seminarians should be allowed to pursue a secular higher education before entering the senior seminary. This decision came as a major surprise. The idea that candidates for the priesthood should temporarily step off the fast track to ordination, and might actually benefit from exposure to the outside world first, seemed genuinely radical. But from my perspective the decision was ideal: if I did well in my A-levels I would be able to go off to university at the end of Higher Line with no questions asked. My two older brothers were already there, and my parents would definitely want me to go as well. At the very least, I should be able to defer for several years the inevitable confrontation with my mother. Or so I thought.

My escape route from Upholland had just been defined. All I needed to do now was make sure that I qualified.

§

The College's greater openness to the outside world was evident in other respects as well. The common rooms were now equipped with radios (which were tuned most of the time to the BBC's new pop music station, Radio One). Higher Line boys were allowed to join a national movement known as the Young Christian Students, and to interact with YCS members from other schools; some even traveled into nearby Wigan to help at the local Oxfam shop. The biggest and most welcome change, however, was an end to the tradition of spending Christmas at the seminary. Autumn term 1967 ended on December 23, and for the first time in six years I was able to spend Christmas at home with my family.

As the school year wound down we were excited by yet another example of our greater freedom to interact with our secular peers. In collaboration with other YCS groups in the area, we helped to organize a sponsored walk from Manchester to Liverpool that would take place early in the summer vacation. When the day came and we had trudged about half of the thirty-five miles, we were beginning to regret the teenage machismo that had prompted us to choose such a long distance. But we could only savor the metaphorical distance Upholland had come in allowing us to collaborate with the event's other organizers.

§

After another summer working for my father, ogling and being tantalized by the girl in the front office, I returned to Upholland in September 1968 determined that the upcoming year would be my last as a seminarian. As the mid-term break approached, I began to think seriously about my application to attend university the following year, which I would need to submit in December. By now my parents knew of my intention to apply, although not of my longer-term plans beyond graduation. While I was home for the break we had several discussions about the application process, which they understood well from their recent experience with my two older brothers.

Back at Upholland the chemistry teacher, Fr. Short, was also providing invaluable advice, not least by introducing me to a subject I had never encountered before that quickly became my chosen field of study: biochemistry. He continued to help as I tackled the next step in the process, which was to choose the six universities I would be required to specify on the "UCCA" (common) application form, and then to rank them in order of preference. Had the authorities not decided that seminarians could benefit from a secular higher education, there were would have been no way for me to apply to university while still at Upholland. Fr. Short would not have been available to help me, and I could not have attended the interviews that were part of the universities' selection process.

My final list of six universities was a peculiar mix. My own knowledge of the higher education system was minimal, and although Fr. Short knew rather more, he didn't realize he was advising me on a career-defining choice rather than a temporary detour on my path to the priesthood. Only one of my six choices would be on the list if I were compiling it again today. Fortunately this was the one I decided to name as my first choice, largely because it offered the opportunity to live in the nation's capital city. So when I filled out the UCCA application form, top of my list was University College London.

As I sent off my application I would happily have accepted a place at any of the six universities. Although I was anxious to lay the right foundation for a career in science, I was just as concerned about securing my exit from Upholland. The university route would be the least controversial way for me to leave, and I was glad to be making it a reality at last.

§

As the oldest boys in the School, the eight of us still remaining in my class were now "prefects." This gave us significant responsibility for supervising younger boys and maintaining discipline. In previous years only a subset of the students in Rhetoric had been appointed as prefects, and it had been a mark of distinction to be chosen. With our class, however, there were so few of us left that the authorities chose not to discriminate between us, and appointed us all.

One of the perks that came with being prefects was that we had our own common room, small but reasonably comfortable. Its most important feature was its isolated location, high up in the old main wing, at the top of its own small staircase. This gave us a sense of privacy we had rarely enjoyed since arriving at

Upholland, and encouraged open discussions that brought us closer together than we had ever been.

One obvious topic of conversation was the future. As literature about colleges and universities found its way into the common room, we naturally began to discuss our plans. One by one, each of us owned up to deciding against the priesthood; we were all determined to leave Upholland for good. As yet, none of us had informed the College authorities, and so we swore each other to secrecy. From this point forward the common room felt even more like a special haven, a place where we could talk unguardedly about our secular ambitions. The relief of being able to do so was enormous.

§

By this time we enjoyed a freedom of movement outside the College grounds that was inconceivable when we first arrived. On certain days, for example, we were at liberty to catch a bus into Wigan and entertain ourselves in whatever manner we chose. One such jaunt in particular still stands out in my mind. After lunching on fish and chips in the town centre, a few of us sneaked into the local cinema to watch a film called "Candy." This featured Ringo Starr and a host of big-name stars (Marlon Brando, Richard Burton, James Coburn and Walter Matthau among others) hamming their way through a truly ridiculous plot. What grabbed our attention was the nymph-like lead actress with long blonde hair who was ravished by one man after another, most notably by Ringo on a billiard table. We watched in awed but embarrassed silence, our gazes fixed straight ahead for fear of making eye contact with each other. While I do not remember a single word passing between us on the subject afterwards, I am quite convinced that if any of us still harbored thoughts of celibacy by then, this experience must have been killed off them once and for all.

During the Christmas break many of us attended a residential YCS conference at a teacher-training college in Manchester. For most of the attendees this may not have seemed particularly unusual, but for us it was a rare opportunity to mix freely with students of our own age, and especially with girls. In many ways the experience was torture: seminary life had simply not equipped us with the social skills for such a gathering. Thinking back now to some of my conversations there, all I can do is wince.

Luckily not all of my conversations were so embarrassing, and one turned out to have considerable practical value. Talking with one of the organizers of the conference, I learned that the YCS operated a hostel in London for visiting students, and that I would be able to stay there if University College called me for interview. So when in due course that happened, I contacted her and arranged to stay—neatly solving what otherwise would have been quite a logistical challenge. My parents sent me money for the train fare and incidental expenses, and I was all set for the trip.

Leaving Upholland during the middle of term for a solo excursion to London was hugely exciting. Nerve-wracking too, given the reason for the trip. My day at UCL went well, its most memorable event being the personal interview I had with Professor Baldwin, head of the biochemistry department. He was a tall man who sat awkwardly in a deep armchair, seemingly unsure about where exactly to park his unusually long legs. Throughout the interview he kept me fixed in his gaze, which was highly unnerving because his eyes were magnified to an enormous size by his spectacles. He took pains to explain how life at UCL would broaden my mind far beyond the realm of my chosen subject; perhaps because of my background, he commented specifically that students might arrive as Catholics and leave as Buddhists. "That will never be me," I thought, as I listened respectfully, joining in only when my input seemed required.

The contrast with my interview seven years earlier with Archbishop Heenan could not have been greater. But the outcome was similar: a few weeks after my interview I received a letter informing me I had been accepted. This time there were conditions, that I passed three of the A-levels I was taking in the summer. But that was all I had to do, pass them. As the letter explained, UCL liked to encourage strong A-level results by not requiring them. Or perhaps Professor Baldwin really did want to see how I reacted to Buddhism.

§

Back at Upholland I was relishing an unusual degree of solitude. As prefects, my classmates and I each had our own rooms on what had once been the Minors' corridor in the old main wing, but during the first term of my final year I had been assigned to supervise the Higher Line dormitory, which required me to sleep there. After more than three months of struggling to maintain discipline over boys who were almost as old as me, and saw no particular reason to comply when I tried to enforce *magnum silentium* and lights-out, I was glad when the term came to an end and the assignment passed to another prefect. When we returned for the Spring term at the beginning of 1969 I was able to sleep for the first time in my single room, and really reveled in the experience; I had never previously slept in a room that was mine alone.

More important than its privacy, however, was the quiet solitude my room provided for uninterrupted study. For the rest of the year my focus became exactly what UCL had intended: working hard to achieve the best possible results in my A-levels. As the date of the exams loomed ever closer, I became as close to a hermit as the routine of College life would allow.

§

In the few idle moments my revision allowed, I began to wrestle with an important question concerning my future. Should I inform my parents and the College that I would not be returning to Upholland after university, or stay silent on the subject and tell them only when I graduated? Tempting though it was to pursue the latter path, I concluded that I did not want to spend the next three years living under false pretences and assumptions. To do so would have been fundamentally dishonest, and would also have prevented me from enjoying university life to the full; I was anxious to shed the behavioral expectations that would persist if I were technically still a seminarian. The answer was therefore clear. I needed to tell all concerned that I was leaving Upholland for good.

Mindful of my abortive attempt to leave two years earlier, I was determined to ensure that this time my decision would stick. The best way to guarantee this would be to inform the College authorities before I left at the end of the year, and my parents only after I returned home. My mother would then have absolutely no chance of "persuading" me to change my mind.

Informing the College turned out to be relatively painless. One evening after supper I simply knocked on Fr. Cheetham's door, waited for him to ask me in, and gave him the news. Although he expressed disappointment, he did not make any serious attempt to change my mind, only inquiring about my future plans and offering his good wishes. Our entire discussion lasted just a few minutes. I left his room deeply satisfied at having taken such an important step.

The next step would be much more difficult, informing my parents. But that would have to wait. For the moment, I had an even more important matter to attend to: my A-levels.

§

July came, and with it the exams. One last round of frenzied revision, a heart-pounding wait outside the study hall, and I was finally sitting at a desk with the first paper in front of me. Three hours and yards of ink later, the first exam was over. One week and a mile of ink later, they were all over.

So too was my time at Upholland. As I packed my belongings and said farewell to my friends, I could not help feeling a little wistful about this. Enjoyment is not a word I would ever use to describe my experience in the seminary, but I had spent over a third of my life there, so inevitably felt some attachment to the place.

Two thousand five hundred days had passed since I first came up the College drive, full of excitement, awed by my first glimpse of the monumental building. As I now departed for the last time down the same drive, unable to resist one final look back, that excitement had long since died away, to be replaced by a new enthusiasm for a very different future. Only one obstacle remained between me and that future: the daunting task of telling my parents that I had no intention of becoming a priest.

§

The big confrontation happened about two weeks after I returned home. The delay was not just because I needed time to summon up my courage; along with the rest of the world, our family was totally engrossed in the Apollo 11 mission to land the first man on the Moon. Until this was over, it would have seemed sacrilegious to spoil the atmosphere with what was bound to be an acrimonious discussion.

Ten days after I left Upholland, Neil Armstrong took a small step onto the Moon's surface and declared it a giant leap for mankind. The time was four in the morning in Liverpool, but like people everywhere we were glued to the TV, transfixed by the amazing images from space. Just a few days later it was my turn to take a small step that felt like a giant leap. Mine required less bravery, although almost as much as I could muster. After mentally rehearsing my lines for the umpteenth time, I asked my parents if I could talk to them in the sitting room. Pressing ahead before I could lose my nerve, I rushed through my prepared speech: that after thinking about it for a long time I had decided I did not want to become a priest, and so would not be returning to Upholland after I graduated from university; I had been feeling this way for several years, so my decision was not sudden or impetuous; what it was, though, was firm and final—I had already informed Fr. Cheetham.

My mother's reaction was almost exactly what I had expected and feared. After a brief period of calm while she processed the news, she harangued me with every reason she could imagine to make me change my mind, and turned increasingly angry when I refused to budge. How could I throw away the last seven years of my life? Hadn't I always wanted to be a priest? How could I take such an important decision without consulting her? Didn't I realize how upset she would be? How dare I present her with a *fait accompli*, telling her only after informing the College authorities? And so on.

In defending myself I was greatly handicapped by the sheer impossibility of mentioning the most important reason for my decision; it was simply out of the question to tell her that I was too interested in girls to contemplate a life of celibacy. The closest I came, after she recited her litany of objections yet again, was to point out forcefully that *I* was the one who would have to live the life of a priest, not her, and that I simply did not want to do so.

Still she came back at me, until eventually (and unwittingly) I said something that shut down the discussion for good. Invoking the name of an older brother whom she regarded as a disrespectful rebel—mainly because of heated disagreements over curfews and other limits—I commented that I now understood exactly how he felt. For her erstwhile "golden boy" to side with her oft-declared "black sheep" was more than my mother could stand. She stormed out of the room in a giant huff, and did not speak to me again for weeks. My father tried to intercede on her behalf, but I gave him the same message I had given her: this was *my* life we were talking about, not hers, and I was not going to live as a priest just to please her.

As the weeks went by and it became clear that I was not going to change my mind or apologize for my position, my mother begrudgingly allowed herself to accept it. By the time my A-level results arrived in late summer, confirming that I would shortly be leaving for university, we were on full speaking terms again. With peace declared at home, I could finally consider my Upholland experience to be over, and look forward with eagerness to my future. No longer was I destined to be a priest; London and biochemistry beckoned me. I had no idea where they would lead me, but was absolutely convinced it would be exciting. And so it has proved to be.

CHAPTER 8

SWUNG BY THE SIXTIES?
UNDERSTANDING THE ABUSE EPIDEMIC

During my years at Upholland, the idea that a priest might molest a child would have been almost unthinkable. Yet by the time I left the seminary in 1969, hundreds of priests in the US were doing precisely that; the incidence of such behavior among the clergy had in fact been climbing steadily for almost twenty years. Nobody was aware of this, however, because most victims waited many years before reporting what had happened to them. For the same reason, nobody noticed when the epidemic of abuse began to recede about a decade later. Only when the *Nature and Scope* report was published in 2004 did the full chronology of the abuse epidemic emerge: the steady climb between 1950 and 1980, and the sharp decline thereafter.

This chronology raises puzzling questions, the answers to which are crucial to understanding why the epidemic occurred and what brought it to an end—and therefore to ensuring that it is never repeated.

The first puzzle hinges on the widely accepted view, which I share, that traditional seminary training played a major role in predisposing certain priests to commit abuse. But why then did the incidence of abuse suddenly begin to climb in the 1950s? Seminary training at that time was still the same as it had been for generations, yet by the end of the decade the incidence of abuse was over six times higher than it had been at the beginning, and had already risen to almost half of the peak figure reached in 1980. Had this climb begun in the late 1960s it would have been much easier to understand, given the sexual and social revolutions then taking place. But in the 1950s, traditional moral and social values still largely prevailed. So again, why did priests trained in the same way as their predecessors suddenly begin to ignore these traditional values and to molest children? And how can the circumstances that led them to do so be avoided in the future?

If the beginning of the abuse epidemic is a puzzle, so too is the end. In 1981, after climbing almost continuously for three decades, the incidence of abuse began to fall. By 1984 it had already tumbled over 40 percent from its peak four years earlier; ten years later it was down to levels last seen in 1952. What makes this puzzling is that the decline began several years before the Church even realized it had a major problem, and long before it had taken any steps to respond. Until late 1984, when Fr. Gilbert Gauthé of Louisiana became the first priest anywhere to be indicted on sexual abuse charges, few people beyond those directly involved were aware that priests were molesting children. Indeed, the statistics now available show that prior to the publicity generated by the Gauthé case, the great majority of abuse by priests had gone unreported: more than 11,000 incidents are now known to have occurred during the 35-year period between 1950 and 1985, but only 810 of them had been reported by the end of that period. Mathematically, this means that the average diocese would have received only one complaint every six years or so—which is why Church leaders had not yet realized the scale of the problem or the need to address it. But if that was still the situation in 1985, and indeed for a number of years thereafter, why did the incidence of abuse begin to fall so precipitously around 1980? And what pointers does the fall provide for the prevention of abuse in the future?

EARLIER EXPLANATIONS

Despite its importance, few previous analyses have paid much attention to the chronology of the abuse epidemic. Most have focused on the appalling response of Church authorities to incidents of abuse: the unsympathetic treatment of victims, the lenient handling of their molesters, the deplorable practice of moving known abusers to new parishes, the secret settlements. A subset of theses analyses have delved into the reasons why priests engaged in abusive behavior, the most common view being the one alluded to above, that this was a consequence of arrested emotional development induced by the closed and repressive environment of the seminary. But only a few have given much consideration to the timing of the epidemic, and what this reveals about its causes.

The first thorough attempt to explain the chronology was the 2004 report by the National Review Board, which cited a number of developments that it felt had contributed to the origins and growth of the epidemic. These included a boom in seminary enrolment during the 1950s, which overwhelmed the capacity of Church authorities to screen candidates adequately, and thus allowed a larger number of unsuitable individuals into the priesthood; the aftermath of Vatican II reforms, which were seen as weakening the absolute moral certainties of the past; the impact of the "sexual revolution" in secular society that began in the mid-to-late 1960s; the "culture of dissent" within the Church that developed in response to *Humanae vitae*, the 1968 papal edict reaffirming the ban on artificial contraception; and a "gay subculture" that took hold in certain seminaries during the 1970s and 1980s.

On first impression these conclusions seem quite convincing, particularly since they largely coincide with views expressed by several other well-informed commentators on the abuse crisis. They therefore warrant serious consideration, even though—for reasons that will shortly be explained—most do not stand up to closer inspection.

One particularly relevant and thoughtful commentator is Father Howard P. Bleichner, the former rector of two prestigious American seminaries, whom we first met in Chapter 4. In his book *View from the Altar: Reflections on the Rapidly Changing Catholic Priesthood,* Fr.Bleichner describes himself as having been "up to my ears in priestly formation since Vatican II," and then goes on to recount the Council's dramatic impact on the formation process. The great strength of the traditional seminary, he notes, was its strictly regimented environment; the seminary "deliberately cultivated the quality of an igloo, a place frozen in time," and treated celibacy as "a discipline descended from on high" that required no discussion or explanation. But when Vatican II instigated change, the strength of this approach became its great weakness: the ramrod discipline inside seminaries was too inflexible to accommodate even moderate reform, in the face of which it simply collapsed.

Fr. Bleichner likens this collapse to the loss of electricity that allowed the dinosaurs to escape in *Jurassic Park*, and argues that in some of those who escaped the seminary as priests, the electric fence that controlled their personal behavior was also switched off; in consequence, these men became the first wave of perpetrators in the abuse epidemic. As seminaries then moved into a mode that emphasized personal growth over strict discipline, sexual experimentation by students was tolerated—thereby allowing a second wave of future abusers to enter the priesthood. And because of the prevailing wisdom that the requirement for priestly celibacy would soon be dropped, nobody had the energy or appetite to go in and tackle the obvious problems that were developing within the seminary system.

Given that his book was published very shortly after the NRB and *Nature and Scope* reports in 2004, Fr. Bleichner clearly wrote much of his analysis before seeing those documents. He did, however, briefly describe their main findings as he wrapped up his discussion of the abuse crisis, and in the process slightly re-cast his arguments about Vatican II. He still saw the Council as a pivotal event that had created two main cohorts of abusive priests, but revised the way in which the first of these cohorts was defined. Rather than products of the disciplinary collapse that followed Vatican II, its members were now defined as priests ordained in earlier decades who felt emboldened by the post-Conciliar climate to pursue whatever abusive instincts they harbored. The second cohort he defined in the same way as previously: men ordained in the 1970s who had experienced few restraints on their behavior in post-Vatican II seminaries. The first group he characterized as having had inhibitions they then lost; the second, as never having had inhibitions in the first place.

In describing the lack of discipline in post-Conciliar seminaries, Fr. Bleichner makes passing reference to the lenient attitude toward homosexual encounters between students, or even between students and faculty members. This observation is consistent with another of the conclusions drawn by the NRB report, namely that a "gay subculture" which developed in certain seminaries during the 1970s and 1980s was a significant contributor to abusive behavior by priests. Several other commentators have made much of this gay subculture and its impact on the priesthood, most notably the Catholic journalist, Michael S. Rose. In the book *Goodbye, Good Men: How Liberals Brought Corruption into the Catholic Church*, Rose argued persuasively that since Vatican II, the "Good Men" of his title—orthodox heterosexual men who aspire to be priests—have been driven away from seminaries by a liberal agenda and the aforementioned gay subculture. The connection he drew between the latter and abusive behavior by priests was somewhat limited by the timing of his book, which came out in 2002 just after the scandals began to rock Boston—giving him barely enough time for a hasty revision to the introduction, in which he suggests that his findings represent at least part of the explanation for abuse by priests.

The tolerance of homosexuality in post-Vatican II seminaries was also highlighted by Leon Podles is his mammoth work *Sacrilege: Sexual Abuse in the Catholic Church*, published in 2008. As befits a former FBI investigator, Podles spends considerable time reviewing the evidence and constructing his case about each of the issues he considers; the gay subculture within seminaries is only one of many factors he cites in indicting homosexuality among priests as a primary cause of the crisis. His case also relies on other arguments that are likely to be much more controversial, for example that "the dynamics of homosexual development lead to a greater proportion of homosexuals as compared with heterosexuals who are attracted to minors"; that "the involvement of men in their forties and fifties with teenage boys suggests that one type of homosexuality is developmentally caused, that somehow these men never matured"; and that "gays themselves have recognized that immaturity seems to be more characteristic of gays than of heterosexuals." These arguments are significantly less compelling than one plain fact cited by Podles from the *Nature and Scope* report's census of abuse complaints: that eighty-one percent of all victims during the abuse epidemic were male.

To wrap up this brief survey of independent commentary on issues related to the timing of the epidemic, we will return to *View from the Altar*—this time for Fr. Bleichner's take on *Humanae vitae*, the 1968 encyclical re-affirming the Church's opposition to artificial contraception. Although he does not blame the encyclical directly for causing clerical abuse, as he did in the case of seminary indiscipline, he does argue that it led to a general questioning of the Church's authority on matters of sexual conduct, and thus to an atmosphere in which certain priests found it easier to ignore the basic rules governing such conduct.

Given the credence they have received from the National Review Board and other observers, why not accept the issues just discussed as the prime causes of the abuse epidemic? Because, quite simply, they came along too late to have played that role.

Take, for example, Vatican II. The Council was convened in 1962 and held its final sessions in 1965; apart from minor changes in the liturgy—such as the early switch to English for the Epistle and Gospel during Mass—its reforms took several years to implement. At Upholland, as noted in the previous chapter, the first relaxation in the code of discipline did not occur until 1966, while in the US, Fr. Bleichner cites 1967 as the year when seminary discipline collapsed. Given the long duration of seminary training and the lapse of time that typically occurred between an abuser's ordination and first offence, the impact of these changes on the incidence of abuse would not have been felt until much later. But even ignoring that fact, and supposing that Vatican II reforms had an immediate impact on the behavior of priests already in ministry, this could not explain why the incidence of abuse in 1966—the year *before* the disciplinary collapse—was ten times higher than it had been in 1950, and only one-third lower than its eventual peak figure. Vatican II simply came along too late to have been a primary cause of the abuse epidemic. And if this is true of Vatican II, it is obviously even more true of developments that occurred later, such as the firestorm over *Humanae vitae,* and the rise of the gay subculture in seminaries during the 1970s.

THE *CAUSES AND CONTEXT* REPORT

So what, then, was responsible for initiating and driving the abuse epidemic? The most recent attempt to answer this question, and much the most comprehensive one, came in 2011 with the publication of a second report by the John Jay College of Criminal Justice, *The Causes and Context of Sexual Abuse of Minors by Catholic Priests in the United States, 1950-2010.* The initial reports by the College and the NRB in 2004 had been commissioned by the US Conference of Catholic Bishops at the height of the abuse scandals in Boston two years earlier, and the pressing need for some official view on the crisis did not allow much time for thorough analysis of all the questions that surfaced during the investigation. Recognizing the need for such analysis, in late 2004 the USCCB requested formal proposals for a much more comprehensive study of the causes and context of the crisis. A year later, the team at the John Jay College was selected to perform the new study, and embarked on a five-year program to do so. The end-product of their efforts was released by the USCCB in May 2011, and will henceforth be referred to by the abbreviated title preferred by its authors, the *Causes and Context* report.

With eight additional years of data about abuse complaints, the new report confirmed the basic "shape" of the epidemic uncovered by the John Jay team's earlier work: most of the abuse reported in the interim dated back several decades, and fit within the temporal pattern previously described. The report also concurred with the view of the National Review Board and numerous other commentators that the traditional, repressive, system of seminary training had left priests ill-prepared to cope with the demands of celibacy, a "vulnerability" that led certain of these priests to commit abuse.

Many of its other findings, however, were somewhat controversial, appearing to absolve the Church of much of the blame it had been allotted by the NRB in 2004. Whereas the Board had been unequivocal in blaming seminaries for failing to screen and form candidates properly, the new report concluded that meaningful screening would not have been possible, and that while priests had indeed been poorly formed, it was the "permissive society" that caused them to come unstuck.

More specifically, the abuse epidemic was now characterized as a "period effect," its rise the result of the rapidly changing social climate during the 1960s and 1970s, and its decline the result of greater awareness about sexual abuse in the early 1980s—although with some credit also due to actions taken by the Church. The great majority of abuse was considered to have been "situational," driven more by the response of priests to their situations than by recognizable psychosexual disorders. Abusers were not significantly more likely than non-abusers to have attended minor seminaries. And because abusers for the most part did not share any readily identifiable characteristics, there was no screening method that could have been used to weed them out before they committed abuse.

The *Causes and Context* report was not well received by the media or the public, who saw it as an attempt by the Church to abdicate responsibility for the crisis—a retreat from the NRB's previous acknowledgment of major deficiencies. The day after the report's release, *Boston Globe* columnist Yvonne Abraham was full of scorn. Under the headline "The Church's Poor Excuse," she began her column with: "The swinging sixties. Seriously? Five years after they began analyzing the causes of sexual abuse by Catholic priests, researchers at John Jay College in New York have come up with a report only a bishop could love." Two days later, a *Globe* editorial proclaimed the report "A Step Backward, Not Forward," criticized it for "beside-the-point semantics," and declared that "by focusing so much on broader trends rather than the specific way the Church handled such accusations, the study comes off as a way of avoiding blame."

This view was presumably reinforced by a series of observations in the report that felt distinctly like excuses. Thus in sending abusive priests for "treatment" and then placing them back into ministry, the Church had been acting in accordance with an accepted view at the time that molesters could be rehabilitated; the poor handling of victims had been due to the lack at that time of any general understanding in society of the harm done by sexual abuse; although some bishops had responded appropriately to cases of abuse in their dioceses, the media had focused on those who did not; celibacy itself had not been the problem, since it remained constant while the epidemic of abuse surged and receded; and so on.

My own initial reaction to the report was that it deserved a better reception than it was receiving. The authors did a remarkable job in assembling and analyzing a huge amount of information on a diverse range of topics, and made a clear case for what they believed to be the appropriate conclusions. The scope and thoroughness of their work were impressive, sufficient to convince me— briefly—that their conclusions were largely consistent with my own experience of seminary life in the 1960s. I even wrote a letter to that effect and e-mailed it to two prominent newspapers. (Neither elected to publish it.)

As I re-read the report several times, however, and dug more deeply into its details, my own reservations grew. These were centered around four main concerns: that the report consistently ignores the crucial early stages of the epidemic, which are surely relevant to understanding its causes; reaches a debatable conclusion about the behavior of priests ordained in different decades; relies on an arbitrary classification scheme for offenders that categorizes as "situational" behavior that most people would call pathological; and implies a greater importance for corrective measures taken by the Church than they warrant, given that abuse was already in steep decline by the time they were introduced.

The Early Stages of the Abuse Epidemic

Throughout the *Causes and Context* report, virtually all references to the timing of the abuse epidemic imply that it started in the 1960s. This pattern is established as early as the second paragraph of the Executive Summary, which states that the authors focused first "on what initiated an increase in abuse incidents in the 1960s; what caused them to reach a peak in the 1970s; and then what led to the sharp and sustained decline in incidence in the 1980s." A few paragraphs later, the very first bullet-point in the itemized list of findings describes the crisis as a "historical problem" in which "the count of incidents per year increased steadily from the mid-1960s through the late 1970s, then declined in the 1980s and continues to remain low." The four other references in the Executive Summary to the timing of the epidemic all count the 1960s as the starting point—as does almost every other such reference in the remaining 120 or so pages of discussion and analysis.

This perspective was clearly reflected in the report's overall conclusions, which were summarized as follows:

> No single "cause" of sexual abuse of minors by Catholic priests is identified as a result of our research. Social and cultural changes in the 1960s and 1970s manifested in increased levels of deviant behavior in the general society and also among priests of the Catholic Church in the United States. Organizational, psychological, and situational factors contributed to the vulnerability of individual priests in this period of normative change.

Or to put it more plainly: although no one factor can be blamed for the crisis, the impact of the Swinging Sixties on poorly prepared priests comes close.

The problem with this conclusion is that, as we have previously noted, the abuse epidemic was well under way before the Swinging Sixties arrived. The evidence for this was already clear in the *Nature and Scope* report in 2004, and is strongly confirmed by the updated data presented in the new report. Even to the naked eye, the graph in Figure 1.1 of the latter clearly indicates that the incidence of abuse began to rise in the 1950s, and rose just as quickly in that decade as in the two that followed.

To quantify this more precisely, I enlarged a copy of the graph in question and carefully read off the data points for each year, and then applied a correction for an artifact noted elsewhere in the report, namely that the data for the years 1950, 1960 and 1970 include all incidents in the corresponding decades that were reported with the year unspecified; the correction simply distributed these incidents among the individual years of the decade in proportion to the actual number of cases reported in each one. Thus transcribed and corrected, the data allow a highly revealing analysis of the growth in the epidemic before and after 1965, which was about the time the social and sexual "revolutions" of the 1960s really got started (and which, coincidentally, was also the final year of the Second Vatican Council). In the fifteen years between 1950 and 1965, the incidence of abuse rose from 61 to 620 cases a year, an increase of 559; in the fifteen years that followed, supposedly the peak years for growth, the corresponding increase was 340 cases a year. In other words, abuse actually grew more quickly *before* the arrival of the permissive society than after it; the arrival did *not* increase the rate at which abuse was climbing.

At the very least, this suggests that the impact of the Swinging Sixties was merely to extend a process whose momentum was already established. A more aggressive but perfectly reasonable interpretation would be that they had no impact at all.

To make sure that the figures just quoted did not simply reflect changes in the total number of priests, I tracked down statistics for the clerical population in the US from 1950 onwards, and then calculated for each year the number of abuse cases reported per thousand priests. The conclusion remained the same. Between 1950 and 1965, this figure grew from 1.42 to 10.57; by 1980, it had reached 16.44. Again, the increase in the fifteen years before the advent of the permissive society was bigger than the increase in the fifteen years that followed.

These conclusions do of course assume that the figures reported to the John Jay College team accurately reflect the actual extent of abuse during the periods in question, which may or may not be a fair assumption. Experts believe that many cases of sexual abuse go unreported; if this was more true of abuse by priests in the 1950s than in subsequent decades, the apparent increase in abuse between 1950 and 1965 could be explained at least in part by a gradual improvement in reporting—in which case the increases before and after 1965 might have been lower and higher, respectively, than they seemed.

Arguing against this, however, is the pattern of reporting described in Chapters 1 and 2 of the *Causes and Context* study. Most incidents of abuse in the decades of interest did in fact go unreported for a very long time; as noted above, although more than 11,000 complaints have now been filed for incidents that occurred between 1950 and 1985, only 810 were on record by the end of that period. The previously unreported cases finally began to emerge during the mid 1980s, presumably in response to the publicity surrounding the Gauthé case in Louisiana, with major surges in reporting during 1993 (the year of a major scandal in Fall River, Massachusetts) and 2002 (the year of the uproar in Boston). Victims from the early 1950s would have been in their mid forties at the time of the Gauthé case and their early sixties during the Boston scandals, and should have been just as able and willing to come forward as victims from later decades. There is thus no reason to suppose that the observations noted above about the pace of the epidemic before and after 1965 were distorted by differential reporting of incidents from different decades. Nor, therefore, is there any reason to doubt the important conclusion to which these observations led: that the epidemic was in full flow well before the permissive society arrived, and was not a product of that development.

The Behavior of Priests Ordained in Different Decades

In concluding that the abuse epidemic was a "period effect" of the 1960s and 1970s, the *Causes and Context* report also relied on a judgment that, irrespective of their dates of ordination, abusive priests all tended to commit abuse during these two decades. The argument went that if abusive behavior by priests depended on their own progression as individuals, its pattern over time would be linked to their lengths of service rather than to the date on the calendar; the incidence of abuse by "ordination cohorts" from different decades would therefore have risen and fallen at different times, rather than together. Whereas, the report concludes, "a cohort-specific pattern is not evident, for each cohort shows an increase and decrease in incidence in the same period"—that period being the 1960s and 1970s.

This conclusion is based on a comparison of three separate graphs in which the pattern of abuse over time is shown separately for each of three different ordination cohorts: priests ordained before 1960, in the 1960s, or in the 1970s. In their commentary on these graphs (Figures 2.8, 2.9 and 2.10 in the report), the authors state that "For each group of men ordained at different times, the participation in sexual abuse of the cohort rises in the 1960s and 1970s and falls in the 1980s." But when I used the same process as before to extract the raw data from these graphs and re-draw them as three separate curves on the same graph, I found myself unable to agree that "a cohort-specific pattern is not evident." The incidence of abuse by the three different cohorts clearly peaked at different times. This became even more obvious when the data were converted to five-year moving averages to smooth out significant "lumpiness" from year to year, as shown in Figure 8.1 (of this chapter, not the report). Judged by these moving averages, sexual misconduct by the three different cohorts peaked in, respectively, 1966, 1974 and 1980, and so was not as synchronous with societal change as the report concluded. Indeed, going back to the raw data for individual years, abuse by pre-1960s priests peaked in 1965, which was before the "sexual revolution" really got started.

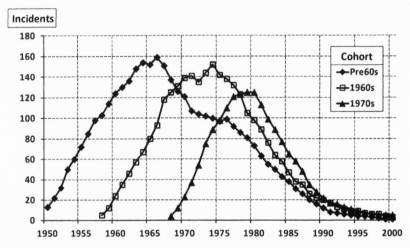

Figure 8.1:   Five-year moving averages for incidence of abuse by priests in different ordination cohorts

On close scrutiny, therefore, whether of the clerical population as a whole or of sub-groups ordained in different decades, the conclusion that the rising incidence of abuse was catalyzed primarily by the social and cultural changes of the 1960s and 1970s simply does not pass muster.

Classification of Offenders

One of the most controversial conclusions of the *Causes and Context* report was that only a small percentage of offender priests were pedophiles. Almost as controversial was the related finding that most abuse was "situational," caused by the intersection of stress and opportunity in priests' lives, rather than by some underlying psychological disorder. The reason these conclusions matter is that they are essential corollaries to the report's overall thesis, that the abuse epidemic was primarily a "period effect" of the Swinging Sixties and their aftermath; this thesis becomes much less convincing if abusers were motivated more by pathological than by situational factors.

Part of the uproar over the pedophilia issue undoubtedly stems from the difference between the popular understanding of this term and its current clinical definition. For many people, anyone who engages in any form of sexual activity with an under-age child is a pedophile. For clinicians, however, as we saw in

Chapter 6, the term is reserved for individuals who experience sustained attraction to pre-pubescent children. If the objects of the attraction are post-pubescent rather than younger, the individual is considered to be an ephebophile—and unlike pedophilia, ephebophilia is not currently classified as a psychiatric disorder (although, as discussed below, the definition of pedophilia may soon be expanded). For the *Causes and Context* report the John Jay team chose to go with the clinical definition, which in the context of their scientific approach to the task at hand, can be seen as a perfectly reasonable decision.

Much less understandable, though, was their decision to define pedophilic behavior even more narrowly than most psychiatrists do. Whereas the reference to "pre-pubescent" children in the current guidelines for diagnosing pedophilia is qualified by the phrase "generally age 13 years or younger," for their most crucial analysis the John Jay researchers chose to apply the pedophile label only to priests who had engaged in sexual activity with a child aged ten or younger—by which criterion, fewer than 5 percent of offender priests were so labeled. But while only 18 percent of victims fell into this arbitrarily chosen age group, 48 percent were aged between eleven and fourteen, and if we assume (since no detailed breakdown is given) that these victims were distributed equally between the four different ages in that grouping, 36 percent of all victims would have been aged between eleven and thirteen. Added to the 18 percent who were aged ten or less, this means that over half of all victims would have fit with the usual clinical definition of pedophilia—strongly suggesting that the percentage of priests who were pedophiles was significantly higher than the figure reported.

Even this calculation, however, does not fully reveal the shortcomings of the scheme used to classify clerical offenders, which is laid out in Table 3.1 of the *Causes and Context* report. To be classified as a "specialist" offender—one driven by an underlying psychological condition—a priest had to meet one of two criteria. Either his victims had to have been exclusively aged ten or younger, in which case he was considered a pedophile; or they all had to have been aged between thirteen and seventeen, in which case he was classified as an ephebophile. Not surprisingly, by these narrow criteria relatively few priests were considered "specialist" offenders: of those who had more than one victim, 3.8 percent met the former definition and 23.9 percent the latter. The remaining 72.3 percent of abusive priests were then classified as "generalists" or "indiscriminate offenders," whose behavior, the report seems to imply, was "situational"—driven by stress and opportunity—rather than pathological. Indeed, a later discussion about the duration and frequency of abuse explicitly states that these parameters were affected by situational rather than psychological factors.

The questionable utility of this classification scheme should be clear from a few examples of behavior patterns that would not be considered pathological by its criteria: abuse of multiple children younger than eleven and one who had reached that age; abuse of multiple eleven- and twelve-year-olds; or abuse of multiple thirteen-year-olds and one child who was younger. Most people would consider all of these behavior patterns pathological, and so would most psychiatrists. But not the *Causes and Context* report.

The idea that abuse driven by a perpetrator's situation should automatically be considered non-pathological is in any case questionable. It implies that only abuse motivated by a "fixated" sexual interest in children (to use the nomenclature explained in Chapter 6) should be considered pathological, and that "regressed" behavior should not be—on the theory, presumably, that this behavior is a temporary aberration induced by an opportunity to molest a child and/or the unavailability of a suitable adult partner, and is therefore unlikely to be repeated. But as the *Causes and Context* report also documents, in many cases of clerical abuse, including many in which the priest had only one victim, the abuse occurred on multiple occasions over a period of about two years. Whatever the motivation for each individual act, it is hard to consider such repeated abuse as anything other than pathological.

The dubious value of the distinctions drawn in the report is made especially clear by pending changes in the guidelines for diagnosing what is currently called pedophilia. In the US, these guidelines are established by the American Psychiatric Association and published in a volume known as the *Diagnostic and Statistical Manual*, or DSM. The Manual is updated periodically to reflect evolving views on psychiatric disorders, with each revision given a new suffix to distinguish it from prior versions; the definition of pedophilia cited above comes from the current version, known as DSM-IV-TR, which dates back to 2000. Amendments for the next revision, to be known as DSM-5, are in an advanced stage of discussion, and the current proposal is to redefine pedophilia as "pedophilic disorder," subdivided into three types—"classic", "hebephilic" and "pedohebephilic" — based on the stage of development of the children to whom the individual is attracted: respectively, prepubescent children, early pubescent children, or both. In the latest draft of DSM-5 (April 2012), the key terms "prepubescent" and "early pubescent" are defined by reference to a standard scale that gauges progression through puberty based on maturational changes in external anatomy. In earlier drafts, however, these terms were defined by reference to the age of the child, with prepubescent meaning "generally younger than 11" and early pubescent "generally age 11 through 14." And while these age-based criteria may now not appear in the final version of DSM-5, their retention in multiple earlier drafts suggests that they must correlate reasonably well with the revised criteria eventually chosen.

In view of which, the planned adoption of DSM-5 in 2013 should eliminate the need for much further debate about the nature of abuse committed by priests: pedophilic or non-pedophilic, situational or pathological? The vast majority of that abuse would be classified unequivocally as pathological—or, to use the synonym that most people have long since given this behavior, just plain "sick." Which, as previously noted, would make it much harder to explain away the epidemic as a product of the Swinging Sixties.

The Cause of the Decline

Also as previously noted, one of the most puzzling aspects of the abuse epidemic was its precipitous decline during the 1980s. The 2004 report from the National Review Board attributed this decline to corrective measures taken by the Church, despite the fact that it pre-dated those measures by a number of years. The 2011 *Causes and Context* report does offer two alternative explanations, without much evidence to support either: a greater awareness in society of the prevalence, causes and consequences of child sexual abuse, and a reduced tolerance in general for "deviant behavior." Consistently, however, it also suggests that the Church's actions played an important role in the decline. The Executive Summary, for example, in only the fifth sentence describing the report's findings, states that "Although no specific institutional cause for the increase in incidence was found, factors specific to the Catholic Church contributed to the decline in the mid-1980s." The impression created by this statement is reinforced by multiple other references. As in the sentence just quoted, the decline is usually described as occurring in the mid-1980s; in one place, as "the sharp decline after 1985." Explanations offered for its cause include "the impact of the events within the Catholic Church." One passage explicitly states that the "decline corresponds to... knowledge of abuse in the church, and implementation of policies to reduce sexual abuse in the church." And in a discussion of improvements to seminary education that took place—at the earliest—in the 1980s, the report suggests that "The addition of elements of what is now called a 'Human Formation' component of seminary education was... consistent with the decline in sexual abuse incidents."

A brief review of the Church's actual actions during the 1980s will make it crystal clear that these could not have been responsible for reversing the tide of abuse. Even after the wake-up call provided by the prosecution of Fr. Gilbert Gauthé in 1984, the Church's response was glutinously slow. This was in spite of strenuous efforts by three people involved in the Gauthé case to alert the National Conference of Catholic Bishops (the predecessor of the USCCB) to the huge liabilities the Church might face because of sexual abuse by priests. The three men in question were Fr. Michael Peterson MD, head of a facility where abusive priests were treated, F. Ray Mouton, the attorney who had represented Gauthé, and Fr. Thomas Doyle, an expert on canon law. Extrapolating from the relatively small number of cases then known, they estimated that the Church could face damages of at least a billion dollars over the next ten years, and recommended a series of actions to deal with the imminent crisis they foresaw. Their proposal, developed entirely on their own initiative early in 1985, was quietly quashed by the NCCB. A committee to work on the problem of priest-pedophilia was promised, but never formed.

In December that year, again on his own initiative, Fr. Peterson circulated the proposal he had developed with Mouton and Doyle to the heads of all dioceses in the US, together with additional advice he had prepared on the handling of abuse cases. This unusual step, even though unofficial, represents the first broad action of any sort within the Church to deal with the abuse problem. But by the time it was taken, the incidence of abuse had already fallen 40 percent from its peak around 1980. Three years later, which is when the NCCB first issued non-compulsory guidelines of its own, the extent of that fall was 63 percent. And by 1992, at which time half of all dioceses had still not implemented a sexual abuse policy, it was 84 percent. Clearly, the decline had little or nothing to do with the Church's intervention.

ALTERNATIVE ACCOUNT

All of which leaves us with a vacuum. Despite its comprehensiveness, the *Causes and Context* report fails to provide convincing explanations for either the rise or the fall of the abuse epidemic—without which we cannot be sure that all appropriate steps have been taken to prevent a recurrence. Better explanations are needed.

The key to finding these, I believe, is a little-discussed aspect of the epidemic that was noted in an earlier chapter: the long delay that typically occurred between an abuser's ordination and first offence. Given the duration of seminary training, this delay meant that the typical offender did not commit his first act of abuse until fifteen to twenty years after entering the seminary. Thus priests who first molested children in the 1950s had begun their training in the late 1930s and early 1940s; those who might have molested children in the early 1980s, but did not, had begun their training in the mid-to-late 1960s. And therein lie the clues to the epidemic's growth and decline.

Consider first the priests who formed the initial wave of abusers in the 1950s and early 1960s. Given that these men had grown up during the Great Depression and the Second World War, at the time they decided to pursue the priesthood they may have seen its hardships as no greater than those of family life. But by the time they were actually ordained, and emerged from eight to twelve years of isolation in seminaries, the world had changed very considerably. Gone were the privations of their youth, superseded by the huge post-War boom in prosperity. All of a sudden, the discrepancy between the hardship of their own lives and the comfort of their parishioners' was much greater than they had expected. And as though to reinforce the point, idealized portrayals of family life were staple fare on the newly ubiquitous medium of television, which was going through its own enormous boom. Almost for the first time, therefore, some of these priests began to realize the full meaning of the lifetime of sacrifice they faced.

Had these priests been of the excellent character traditional for their calling, they might have been able to cope with this realization more effectively. But they also happened to be part of yet another boom: a surge in seminary enrolment that began around 1940, and which (as suggested by the NRB report in 2004) overwhelmed the capacity of Church authorities to screen candidates properly. As a result, a greater number of unsuitable characters entered seminaries, and a greater number were subsequently ordained. When the hardships of the priesthood hit home with these men their commitment to celibacy wavered, but given the detrimental effects of seminary life on their emotional maturity and social skills, they found it difficult to form relationships with adults. Surrounded, in contrast, by young children who idolized them, they found it all too easy to commit abuse. And thus did the epidemic start.

As the 1950s morphed into the 1960s, the rapid change in society and the boom in seminary enrolment both continued. Newly ordained priests therefore continued to find that secular life had moved on considerably while they were isolated in the seminary, and their ranks still included too many unsuitable characters who had slipped through the overloaded screening process. Indeed, as Dr. David Finkelhor suggested after reviewing this chapter, by now the post-war boom and GI Bill may actually have boosted the percentage of such characters among new priests. In earlier times, he argued, the priesthood had attracted many poor but ambitious young men who saw it as their only available avenue for upward social mobility; as these young men now pursued new opportunities created by the changed economic landscape, a higher proportion of those entering seminaries belonged to a second group for whom the priesthood had always had an appeal: individuals who were seeking to escape from sexual difficulties. And if, he went on to conclude, these difficulties were caused by feelings of attraction to other males, this might help to explain why so many victims of clerical abuse were boys (an idea also discussed in Chapter 6).

As the new decade progressed, the increasing openness about sexuality only reinforced the discrepancy between the "hardship gap" priests had expected between themselves and the laity and the gap they were actually experiencing. Still hampered socially and emotionally by the after-effects of their seminary training, the marginal characters among them—including, presumably, many who were refugees from sexual difficulties—continued to resort to children for gratification of their carnal urges. Accordingly, the epidemic continued to grow.

Then, providentially, three developments occurred that would ultimately reverse this unfortunate trend. Ironically, two of these have often been blamed for *causing* the epidemic, and were discussed in that context earlier in this chapter. But their actual effect was precisely the opposite—as we shall now see.

The first of the three developments was the Vatican II-inspired reform of seminaries that began in 1966, and whose major impact at Upholland was described in the previous chapter. By reducing the isolation of seminarians from the outside world, this reform had two important consequences: it allowed future priests to interact more with their secular peers, and so to develop greater social skills, particularly with females; and it meant that they were fully aware of the current state of society, and of the sacrifices they would be making, before they made an irrevocable commitment to the priesthood.

The second welcome development came in the very same year that the reform of seminaries began: their population started to fall, so quickly that by 1970 it was less than half what it had been five years earlier. As a result, greater scrutiny was now possible both of the seminarians who remained and the few candidates who still wanted to enroll. Fewer "bad apples" made it into the priesthood.

The decline in the seminary population was then accelerated by the third major development, the widespread negative reaction to *Humanae vitae*. Traditionally, the main impetus for many Catholic boys to pursue the priesthood had come from their mothers (as it did in my own case). Now, however, disillusioned by the Church's ban on the Pill—a ban imposed on them by a group of celibate males with no comprehension of what it meant to have multiple children and live in constant fear of becoming pregnant again— Catholic women no longer pushed their sons to become priests. Enrolment into seminaries dropped even further. This was particularly true for minor seminaries, almost all of which were forced to close over the next two decades, eliminating the possibility that even the modernized versions of these institutions could predispose additional priests to become molesters.

Because most abusers typically did not commit their first offences until some years after ordination, the beneficial impact of these developments was not immediate; a priest who was halfway through his training when they occurred would still have been about ten years away from the "danger point" at which he might become an abuser. During the 1970s, therefore, the incidence of abuse continued to climb. Indeed, according to a chart in the original *Nature and Scope* report (its Figure 2.3.3), priests ordained in the early part of this decade— shortly after the developments just described—were actually the most likely of all to commit abuse. These men would have started their training under the strict Tridentine system of discipline and finished it under the much looser regimen that followed; for some of them, as Fr. Howard Bleichner observed in *View from the Altar*, the relaxation of seminary discipline was akin to an electric fence being switched off, without which they felt free to venture beyond accepted boundaries of personal conduct. (Not having had the opportunity to scrutinize the *Nature and Scope* data in depth, Fr. Bleichner considered such men to have been the first wave of abusers, whereas they were in fact among the last to participate in the main epidemic.) Moreover, this group of priests may have included the lowest proportion historically of men whose primary sexual interest was in adult females: thousands of priests with that orientation had resigned during the late 1960s and early 1970s to get married, and the same goal and orientation can also be assumed for many of the thousands of would-be priests who bailed out from seminaries during the same period.

By the late 1970s, however, fewer and fewer of the priests reaching the danger point for abusive behavior had received any significant part of their training in Tridentine institutions; more and more were products of the less isolated, less regimented, and less crowded seminaries that had emerged ten years earlier. The incidence of abuse stopped climbing, and then went into sharp and sustained decline. Thankfully, the steady rise that took place over three decades was reversed in only half that time; by 1995 the incidence of abuse was down to the low levels that had preceded the epidemic, and has since declined even further. Long may this continue.

The Evidence

Sixty years after the abuse epidemic began, and eighty years after its initial perpetrators began their training, many of the assumptions built into the foregoing account would be difficult to verify. That said, a variety of analyses will now be presented to support them. These analyses are based in part on data extracted from the two reports prepared by the John Jay College, and in part on information gathered from other sources, such as the statistics about seminaries that have been compiled annually since 1967 by the Center for Applied Research in the Apostolate (CARA) at Georgetown University.

The first analysis, summarized in Figure 8.2 below, very much supports the argument that a surge in seminary enrolment was a key factor in the abuse epidemic—an argument originally advanced by the National Review Board in 2004. The graphic shows how the rise and fall in the US seminary population between 1940 and 1990 eerily foreshadowed the rise and fall in the incidence of abuse by priests, but preceded it by about fourteen years—as might be expected from the duration of seminary training and the previously mentioned delay between ordination and first offence. (Note that statistics about the seminary population in certain periods before 1965 were difficult to find, resulting in several significant gaps in the record; each such gap is bridged in the graph by a dotted straight line between the known figures at either end, which is effectively the same as assuming that the population grew linearly between these figures.)

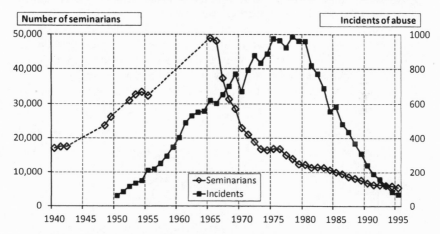

Figure 8.2: Changes in the seminary population and incidence of abuse by priests in the US, 1940-1995

The correlation between the size of the seminary population and the subsequent incidence of abuse is made even more apparent by the next graphic (Figure 8.3 below), which compares the number of incidents each year with the number of seminarians fourteen years earlier—effectively "time-shifting" the data for the seminary population by that number of years. Remarkably, the two curves then fall almost exactly on top of each other, with a high (and statistically

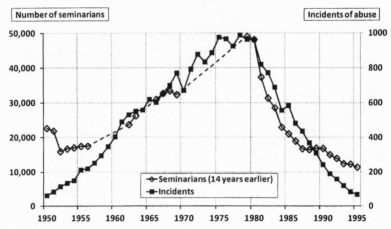

Figure 8.3: Correlation between incidence of abuse and seminary population fourteen years earlier

significant) degree of correlation. The clear implication is that the boom in seminary enrolment was a major factor in the subsequent increase in abuse.

One trivial explanation for this observation would of course be that the boom in enrolment led to more men being ordained, and so to more priests being available to commit abuse. A review of the relevant data, however, quickly disposes of this possible explanation. Between 1950 and 1980 the clerical population grew by a mere 36 percent, very much less than the sixteen-fold increase in the incidence of abuse during the same period. Moreover, when the "abuse rate" (*i.e.*, the number of cases per thousand priests) in each year is compared with the size of the seminary population fourteen years earlier, as shown in Figure 8.4 below, the two parameters show a statistically significant

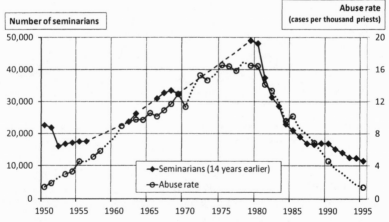

Figure 8.4: Correlation between abuse rate and seminary population fourteen years earlier

degree of correlation, strongly implying that a higher percentage of the seminarians who enrolled during the boom years went on to become abusers. And since these seminarians received essentially the same training as generations of priests before them, the additional implication is that recruiting standards dropped—and that this development contributed significantly to the start of the abuse epidemic.

As for other factors that did or did not contribute to the epidemic, their roles can best be inferred from the final graphic shown below (Figure 8.5). The upper panel of this graphic displays the incidence of abuse in each year between 1950 and 2000, while the lower panel maps out the influences that might have affected the behavior of a priest who reached the seventh anniversary of his ordination in any given year—that anniversary representing the "danger point" at which a typical abuser committed his first offence (with the caveat that the choice of a single anniversary for this analysis, while simplifying the graphic, does lead to some loss of precision; the delay until first offence was generally longer than seven years in the early stages of the epidemic, and shorter in the later stages).

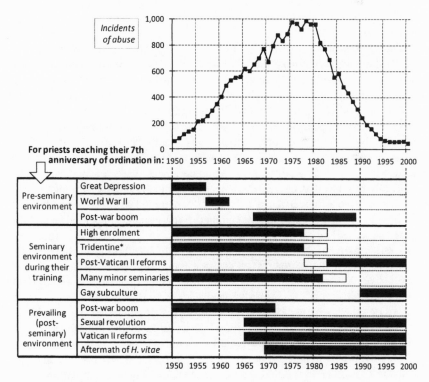

* Environment classified as Tridentine for priests who received at least half their training before 1966 reforms

*Figure 8.5: Chronology of the abuse epidemic and of factors that may have
                   influenced its perpetrators*

Looking first at the seminary environment in which seven-year-priests had been trained (displayed in the central part of the graphic's lower panel), we see that the final climb in the incidence of abuse during the late 1970s occurred just as the final cohort of priests trained in highly populated Tridentine seminaries reached their seventh anniversaries. This cohort would also have been among the last to contain a significant number of former minor seminarians. Then, around 1980, as these priests were followed through the seven-year milestone by the first group trained predominantly in post-Vatican II seminaries, the incidence of abuse began to decline precipitously. Also clear from this part of the graphic is that the development of a "gay subculture" in certain seminaries during the 1970s and 1980s occurred too late to have played much role in the epidemic—which, by the way, was also the conclusion of the *Causes and Context* report.

Turning next to the post-seminary environment experienced by priests as they reached their seventh anniversaries, we see that—as discussed at some length above—the abuse epidemic was well under way before any of the developments in the mid to late 1960s could have influenced it. Vatican II reforms, the sexual revolution, *Humanae vitae*: all came along too late to have initiated the epidemic, and did not significantly increase the rate at which abuse was climbing.

Which takes us back to the question we started with, which is why abuse began to climb as it did during the 1950s and early 1960s. As can clearly be seen by scanning consecutively through the three panels in the lower part of the graphic, the priests who reached the "danger point" in this period had grown up in times of great hardship, entered Tridentine seminaries whose recruiting standards were compromised by high enrolment, and found themselves surrounded by suddenly affluent parishioners when they emerged from their long years of isolation in these institutions—which in many cases they had entered as boys. This combination of experiences was, in my view, the combustible mixture that ignited the abuse epidemic. Tridentine seminaries had always done psychological harm to a small percentage of those who attended them, but that percentage rose as the number of marginal characters accepted for training increased; and unlike potential abusers in previous generations of priests, these more recent marginal characters were faced with an increasingly large gap between the hardships of the priesthood and the comforts in other people's lives—a gap much larger than they had expected when they had entered the seclusion of the seminary, and which constantly reminded them of the sacrifices they were making. Over time, their discontent led them to break their vows of celibacy, which they found easier to do with children than with adults because of the psychological legacy of seminary life. And thus, tragically, did the epidemic begin and grow, driven by that legacy. Then, fortuitously, the reforms of Vatican II dismantled the barriers that had isolated seminarians from the realities of the world, producing a new generation of priests who entered the clerical state with much greater awareness of contemporary society and of the sacrifices they were undertaking—and in consequence, a much lower propensity to commit abuse. The epidemic came to an end; hopefully, never to be repeated.

A particularly sad aspect of this whole sorry saga is that the dangers of isolating seminarians from the world were recognized explicitly by Pope Pius XII even before the epidemic got started, but that no action was taken as a result. In paragraph 86 of his 1950 Apostolic Exhortation, *Menti nostrae,* under the heading "Not Too Much Isolation from the World," Pius cautioned that "if young men—especially those who have entered the seminary at a tender age—are educated in an environment too isolated from the world, they may, on leaving the seminary, find serious difficulty in their relations with... ordinary people." His warning, alas, went unheeded. But even he can have had no idea just how tragic the consequences would be.

Minor Seminaries

One issue the forgoing account did not address in any detail is the role of minor seminaries in the abuse epidemic, which was after all the catalyst for much of my work on this book, as I sought to verify the National Review Board's 2004 conclusion that the "closed culture" inside these institutions may have contributed significantly to abusive behavior by priests.

At first blush, that view seemed to take a hit from the *Causes and Context* report, which concluded that abusive priests "were not significantly more likely than non-abusers to attend minor seminaries." On closer examination, however, this statement turns out to be rather less definitive than it sounds. In this and similar phrases throughout the report, the word "significant/ly" is used in the statistical sense, meaning that two or more sets of data were compared mathematically to determine whether any differences between them were "statistically significant"—a term that is usually reserved for differences that have less than a five percent chance of being due to random variation. But the failure to establish statistical significance in a test of this sort does not necessarily mean that real differences do not exist between the data sets being compared; even in cases where this is true, statistical significance can be difficult to establish when one or more of the data sets is small, and/or certain aspects of the data are unreliable.

Both of these limitations seem to apply to the data about minor seminaries that were available to the *Causes and Context* researchers. The narrative on page 40 of the report describes how data about the seminary training of abusive priests were derived from the survey that had produced the original *Nature and Scope* report in 2004. Of the 4,392 offender priests enumerated in that survey, 1,930 were identified as diocesan priests whose *alma maters* could be classified with certainty into different categories of seminary. And of these two thousand or so priests, only seventy-nine—just over 4 percent—were recorded as having attended minor seminaries. The smallness of this number was presumably the basis for the report's conclusion that "those [priests] educated in minor seminaries were not significantly more likely to have allegations than those educated only in major seminaries."

Was it really true, though, as implied by these figures, that only 4 percent of the offenders had attended a minor seminary? A strong case can be made that the actual percentage was considerably higher. To begin with, the information that came back about offender priests in the *Nature and Scope* survey often seems to have been incomplete, and in many instances may simply have failed to include the fact that a given priest had attended a minor seminary. Of the 4,392 surveys returned, 993 (or about 23 percent) did not include any answer at all to the form's question about seminary training. And even among the 3,399 surveys that did, the answer may have been limited just to the final seminary attended by the subject priest. Without access to the completed survey forms this conjecture would obviously be impossible to confirm, but evidence supporting it can be found on the website BishopAccountability.org, whose mission, as its name implies, is to hold the Church hierarchy accountable for the abuse crisis. To that end, its content includes a database of accused priests, in some cases with copies of diocesan assignment records that include information about seminary training. Although the number of such records is small, the examples typically include only a cursory mention of a single seminary, crammed into a limited space on the record, with no dates attached, and no indication one way or the other whether the institution named was the only or just the final seminary attended. These records may not of course be representative of the information used to answer the question about seminary training in the *Nature and Scope* survey, but combined with the considerable number of surveys that came back with that question unanswered, they do suggest that record-keeping about priests' training was often incomplete. So the low percentage of minor seminarians reported in the *Causes and Context* analysis cited above may not accurately reflect the actual percentage of abusive priests who fell into that category.

To obtain a better estimate of the actual percentage, we can first try to determine the overall percentage of priests (abusive or not) who attended minor seminaries, and then make the assumption that these priests were at least as likely to engage in abusive behavior as those who began their training as adults.

Several sources suggest that a good proportion of all priests did in fact attend minor seminaries. As noted in Chapter 6, a study of six thousand priests conducted by the National Opinion Research Center at the start of the 1970s reported that three-fifths of American clergy graduated from high school before entering a seminary—suggesting that the other two-fifths must have attended minor seminaries. This figure is consistent with the annual statistics that Georgetown University's CARA began compiling in 1967, which showed that "high school seminarians" constituted around 40 percent of the seminary population at that time. A few years earlier that percentage had been even higher: according to statistics quoted in the 1960 *Official Catholic Directory*, it was 63 percent. And while the drop-out rate was probably higher among these younger seminarians than among their older counterparts, these figures strongly suggest that the proportion of priests who attended minor seminaries was rather higher than 4 percent.

That was certainly the case in the one diocese for which I can produce a verifiable figure, which unfortunately for the present purpose was on the other side of the Atlantic: the archdiocese of Liverpool. Once (or occasionally twice) each year, the seminary I attended published the *Upholland Magazine*, which invariably included lists of the previous year's new students and ordinations. By consulting the nearly complete set of issues published between 1935 and 1975 that is held in the archdiocesan archive, I was able to compile a database of over 1,500 seminarians who attended Upholland during that period, and to determine the point at which each newly ordained priest had entered the seminary. About half of all Upholland's new priests came from dioceses other than Liverpool, and typically entered the College as major seminarians; because the *Magazine* did not record whether these individuals had attended a minor seminary in their home diocese, they were excluded from the analysis. Liverpool priests, on the other hand, would all have attended Upholland for the entirety of their training (with occasional exceptions who went off to the English Colleges in Rome or Vallodolid). Among those ordained in the 1940s, 92 percent had begun in the minor seminary, while for the 1950s and 1960s the corresponding figures were 76 percent and 62 percent. These figures may or may not be representative of priests ordained in the US during these decades; although (as we saw in Chapter 4) seminaries in the US and the UK operated in essentially the same way, many external factors unique to the respective countries may have influenced the attrition rate among seminarians. Nonetheless, the data from Upholland do support the general impression from other sources that the proportion of US priests who began their training in minor seminaries was considerably higher than 4 percent.

Assuming that this was indeed the case, it would then be reasonable to infer that the percentage of *abusers* who experienced these institutions was also significantly higher than the 4 percent suggested by responses to the *Nature and Scope* survey. As noted in Chapter 6, many of the factors thought to predispose adults to abusive behavior are experiences that occur during adolescence; given the isolated and repressive environment inside Tridentine minor seminaries, future priests who attended them would have been just as likely, if not more, to undergo these experiences as those who still lived with their families during adolescence, and therefore just as likely to become abusers. In which case, minor seminarians should have constituted at least as high a percentage of abusers as they did of the overall clerical population—with their abusive tendencies the direct result of their early seminary experiences.

By this logic, minor seminaries did indeed play an important role in the abuse epidemic; in some fraction of their students, the "closed culture" bemoaned by the NRB had planted the seeds of future abusive behavior. That culture, fortunately, began to disappear after Vatican II. So too did minor seminaries themselves, as the sexual revolution and the disillusionment of Catholic mothers over *Humanae vitae* led to drastically reduced enrolment. In 1967, the first year CARA compiled its statistics, there were 15,823 high-school seminarians in the US; ten years later, the number had plummeted to 6,069, and by 2010 it was just 532.

§

Within this chapter's conclusions about the abuse epidemic lie terrible ironies. Four centuries earlier, the isolation of future priests in seminaries remote from society was conceived as a way to *eradicate* clerical misconduct: the corruption and lax morals that had long provoked resentment among the laity, and thereby helped to fuel the Reformation. That resentment was also based in part on the contrast between the relative comfort enjoyed by clerics and the hardship endured by many of the laity whose tithes supported them. Now, the very isolation that was supposed to eliminate clerical misconduct had encouraged it, in part because of the contrast between the sudden comfort enjoyed by the laity and the continuing hardship endured by priests. This reversal in circumstances catalyzed an accidental but horrible reverse alchemy: the golden reform that had rescued the Church from the first major crisis in its history was transformed into the lead weight that dragged it into the second.

If there are unfortunate ironies in the origins of the abuse epidemic, there are much more fortunate ones in its decline. Both of the steps taken by the Church that led to this decline were taken for reasons completely unrelated to the epidemic, and in complete ignorance of its existence and causes. The reforms that ended the extreme isolation of seminarians were prompted not by any concern that this was predisposing certain priests to commit abuse, but by the modernizing spirit of the Second Vatican Council. And Pope Paul VI certainly had no intention of facilitating better scrutiny of would-be priests, and of eliminating almost all minor seminaries, when he refused to sanction the use of the Pill; these beneficial developments were fortuitous consequences of the disillusionment he caused among Catholic mothers with his ruling. Thus the end of the abuse epidemic, like its beginning, was an accident of Church policy. In this case, however, the irony is much more welcome.

§

According to the famous epigram coined by Spanish philosopher George Santayana, those who cannot remember the past are condemned to repeat it. The foregoing analysis gives good reason to hope that the abuse epidemic is indeed a thing of the past—especially given the additional protections introduced by the Church since the 2002 scandals—but also suggests three important lessons that should not be forgotten in the quest to prevent abuse by priests in the future.

First, the clamor in certain quarters for a return to pre-Vatican II traditions in the Church should be strongly resisted. Many conservative commentators firmly believe that the entire abuse crisis should be blamed on the Second Vatican Council, and hanker for the unapologetic authoritarianism and uncompromising moral dictates of the pre-Conciliar Church. But at least as far as seminary training is concerned, the events of the late twentieth century have shown that the sixteenth-century tradition established by the Council of Trent was dangerously outmoded in today's rapidly changing world. The way to produce priests who can sustain their vows is not by shielding seminarians as much as possible from "the pleasures of the world"; only when they fully understand what they are relinquishing can seminarians make a truly informed decision to proceed with ordination.

Second, the Church needs to take deliberate steps to ensure that it keeps abreast with changes in society as they develop. In many ways the Church is like a large multi-national corporation, and it would do well to learn from the case-studies taught in many business schools about formerly successful corporations that failed to anticipate and adapt to change. For centuries, Tridentine seminaries had been a major success story for the Church, justly admired for restoring the reputation of the priesthood and for the quality of the priests they produced. But when society underwent one seismic shift after another—the Great Depression, the Second World War, the post-war boom, the rapid spread of television—these institutions carried on in much the same way as they always had, determinedly ignoring the huge changes taking place all around them. And what did they produce as a result? Priests who were unable to adapt to the changed society in which they found themselves, and ended up molesting children. Granted, only a small minority of priests went down this path, but that is no consolation; the harm they did to their victims and to the Church has been immeasurable. Pope John XXIII clearly understood that the Church needed to adapt to the modern world, and now appears visionary in having called the Second Vatican Council almost immediately after his election. That clarity of vision about the impact of societal change has rarely been apparent in the decades since—during which society has undergone yet further radical change. Regular objective reviews of the current relevance of Church policies relating to seminary training, sexual abuse, and many other issues should be mandatory. And just like major corporations who bring in independent consultants to critique their business practices and strategies, the Church should engage outside experts to conduct its periodic reviews of internal policies and their implementation.

To different extents, local hierarchies in a handful of countries—typically those that have experienced major scandals—are already exercising vigilance of the sort just advocated. This is most true in the US, where the USCCB quickly adopted the *Charter for the Protection of Children and Young People* during the 2002 abuse scandals, and has since been diligent in updating and implementing it (which in no way excuses the earlier failures of American bishops to protect minors). The Charter itself has been revised twice, and independent nationwide audits of compliance with its provisions have been conducted in each of the last nine years—all under the watchful eye of the lay National Review Board, whose members are independent experts in a variety relevant issues. Outside the US, mandates and oversight committees similar to the Charter and the NRB have been established in at least two other countries, Ireland and the United Kingdom, and investigative commissions in several more, although none of these initiatives has yet matched the scale and implementation of the USCCB program.

But while local programs are clearly essential, sexual abuse by priests is a global problem; as of May 2012, Wikipedia listed twenty-seven different countries in which abuse scandals have occurred. The Church therefore needs to take global action to ensure that its policies (and their local implementation) are subject to regular and realistic review, with input from outside experts. That action can only come from the Vatican—which unfortunately means it may never occur. Popes John Paul II and Benedict XVI may both have issued public apologies to victims of abuse, but in terms of concrete reforms, the Vatican's response to the crisis has been limited. This is hardly surprising given the prominent role played in such matters by the Congregation of the Doctrine of the Faith (CDF), a body once headed by Pope Benedict and not exactly known for its responsiveness to change or receptivity to outside input. A case in point is the most recent update to canon law (the revised *Normae de gravioribus delictis*, introduced in 2010), which still requires that all disciplinary proceedings against allegedly abusive priests anywhere in the world must be approved by the CDF. The prospects of this body embracing any external review process seem truly minimal. But until the global Church follows the example of its American branch and adopts such a process, it cannot claim to have taken all reasonable steps to reduce the risk of abusive behavior by priests.

The third major lesson to be drawn from the present analysis of the abuse epidemic is that the Church needs to substantially revise its teachings about sex. In their long-held current incarnation, these teachings are completely unrealistic about human nature and attach disproportionately severe penalties to behaviors that are perfectly natural and harmless. To take one obvious example, masturbation is an activity in which the vast majority of human males engage, including (according to the work of Richard Sipe cited in Chapter 6) a great many priests. But according to the Church, this harmless activity is a mortal sin, subject to exactly the same penalty—eternal damnation—as such heinous acts as rape, armed robbery and murder. So too are "impure thoughts," any potentially arousing thoughts about sexual objects or activities that are not immediately banished as soon as the thinker becomes aware of them. The stress caused by trying to avoid these completely natural activities, and the searing guilt induced by failing to do so, were in my view major factors in arresting the psychosexual development of many future abusers. And for what? The idea that such behaviors should be sins at all, let alone subject to the same spiritual penalties as capital crimes, seems absurd. Much good could be done by the Church acknowledging this absurdity and decriminalizing many natural expressions of human sexuality that it has long condemned.

None of the three lessons just drawn from the abuse epidemic relates specifically to homosexuality or to celibacy. Despite views to the contrary among conservatives (in the case of the former) and liberals (in the case of the latter), there is no evidence that either of these issues was, in and of itself, a primary driver of the abuse epidemic. To be sure, the great majority of victims were male, and the priesthood may have contained a disproportionate number of troubled gay men, but the *Causes and Context* report presents abundant evidence (in this case solid) that homosexual priests were no more likely than their heterosexual counterparts to engage in abuse; moreover, experts seem to agree that an abuser's choice of victim can be influenced as much by opportunity as by sexual orientation. And while the difficulties of the celibate state clearly contributed significantly to the discontent that caused certain priests to become abusive, the low incidence of abuse prior to the 1950s and since the mid 1990s clearly demonstrates that celibacy was not by itself responsible for the epidemic. Abolition of the celibacy requirement might be advisable for other reasons, such as to solve the shortage of priests, but would not automatically prevent clerical abuse in the future.

§

Entering Upholland in 1962, I could never have imagined that half a century later, the priesthood so revered in my family would have done so much damage to so many young lives. Nor could have I imagined that my own imminent experiences might help to explain why this happened. By chance, the seven years I spent in the seminary were divided almost equally between the anachronistic training regimen that caused the epidemic and the post-Vatican II environment that curtailed it. My sincere hope is that the insights provided by these experiences have indeed thrown light on abusive behavior by priests, and will help in some small way to prevent such behavior in the future. The abuse epidemic may be over, but the harm done to victims is lifelong and incalculable. Let there be no more.

BIBLIOGRAPHY

American Psychiatric Association. "DSM-5 Development: Proposed Revision, U 03 Pedophilic Disorder." Accessed June 12, 2012. http://www.dsm5.org/ProposedRevision/Pages/proposedrevision.aspx?rid=186#.

Barnard, Henry, ed. "Episcopal Seminaries—Council of Trent," *American Journal of Education* 1, no. 2 (1876): 289-92. Accessed March 31, 2012. http://books.google.com/books.

Barry, Patrick. *The Penal Laws: Understanding the Era of the Eighty-Five Martyrs.* L'Osservatore Romano, 30 November 1987. Accessed March 31, 2012. http://www.ewtn.com/library/CHISTORY/PENALAWS.HTM

Bellitto, Christopher M. *The General Councils: A History of the Twenty-One Church Councils from Nicaea to Vatican II.* New York/Mahwah, N.J.: Paulist Press, 2002.

Berry, Jason. *Lead Us Not into Temptation: Catholic Priests and the Sexual Abuse of Children,* New York: Doubleday, 1992.

Bleichner, Howard P. *View from the Altar: Reflections on the Rapidly Changing Catholic Priesthood.* New York: The Crossroad Publishing Company, 2004.

BishopAccountability.org. "Assignment Records of Accused Priests." Accessed March 31, 2012. http://app.bishop-accountability.org/member/psearch.jsp?op=assignments.

Boston Globe. "Spotlight Investigation: Abuse in the Catholic Church." Accessed March 31, 2012. http://www.boston.com/globe/spotlight/abuse/.

Boston Globe, Investigative Staff of. *Betrayal: The Crisis in the Catholic Church.* New York: Back Bay Books, 2003.

Center for Applied Research in the Apostolate, Georgetown University. "Frequently Requested Church Statistics." Accessed March 31, 2012. http://cara.georgetown.edu/CARAServices/requestedchurchstats.html.

Christian Web Foundation. "Theopedia: An Encyclopedia of Christianity; Catholic Reformation." Accessed March 31, 2012. http://www.theopedia.com/Catholic_Reformation.

Clancy, Graham and Michael Saini, "Sexual Abuse by Clergy." In *Sex Offenders: Identification, Risk Assessment, Treatment, and Legal Issues,* edited by Fabian M. Saleh, Albert J. Grudzinskas, John M. Bradford, and Daniel J. Brodsky. New York: Oxford University Press, 2009.

Collinson, Patrick. *The Reformation: A History.* New York: Modern Library, 2006.

Comerford, Kathleen M. *Ordaining the Catholic Reformation: Priests and Seminary Pedagogy in Fiesole, 1575-1675*. Firenze: Leo S. Olschki, 2001.

Cornwell, John. *Seminary Boy*. New York: Image, 2007.

Cozzens, Donald. *Secret Silence: Denial and the Crisis in the Church*. Collegeville, Minnesota: Liturgical Press, 2002.

Dokecki, Paul R. *The Clergy Sexual Abuse Crisis: Reform and Renewal in the Catholic Community*. Washington D.C.: Georgetown University Press, 2004.

Dowley, Tim, John H. Y. Briggs, Robert Lindner, David F, Wright, eds. *Introduction to the History of Christianity*. Rev. ed. Minneapolis: Fortress, 2002.

Doyle, Peter. *Mitres & Missions in Lancashire: The Roman Catholic Diocese of Liverpool, 1850-2000*. Liverpool: The Bluecoat Press, 2005.

Doyle, Thomas P. *A Very Short History of Clergy Sexual Abuse in The Catholic Church*. Accessed March 31, 2012. http://www.crusadeagainstclergyabuse.com/htm/AShortHistory.htm.

———. *A Short History of* The Manual. In "Jay's Nelson's Priests of Darkness Article Archive." Accessed March 31, 2012. http://archives.weirdload.com/manual.html.

Doyle, Thomas P., A. W. Richard Sipe, and Patrick J. Wall. *Sex, Priests, and Secret Codes: The Catholic Church's 2,000-Year Paper Trail of Sexual Abuse*. Los Angeles: Volt Press, 2006.

Encyclopaedia Britannica, "Reformation, The." In *Encyclopaedia Britannica*, 11th ed., Vol. 23, 4-22. New York: The Encyclopaedia Britannica Company, 1911. Accessed March 31, 2012. http://books.google.com/books.

———, "Trent, The Council Of." In *Encyclopaedia Britannica*, 11th ed., Vol. 23, 543-52. New York: The Encyclopaedia Britannica Company, 1911. Accessed March 31, 2012. http://books.google.com/books.

Estep, William Roscoe. *Renaissance and Reformation*. Grand Rapids, Michigan: William B. Eedrmans Publishing Company, 1986.

Ferro, Jeffrey. *Sexual Misconduct and the Clergy*. New York: Facts on File, 2005.

Finkelor, David. *Child Sexual Abuse: New Theory & Research*. New York: The Free Press, 1984.

Finkelor, David and associates. *A Sourcebook on Child Sexual Abuse*. Newbury Park, California: Sage Publications, 1986.

Fogler, Jason M., Jillian C. Shipherd, Erin Rowe, Jennifer Jensen and Stephanie Clarke, "A Theoretical Foundation for Understanding Clergy-Perpetrated Sexual Abuse," *Journal of Child Sexual Abuse* (2008) 17: 301-28.

Gallie, D. A. *A Brief History of St Edmund's College*. Accessed March 31, 2012. http://www.stedmundscollege.org/managed_assets/files/College_History.pdf.

Gautier, Mary L. *Catholic Ministry Formation Enrollment: Statistical Overview for 2010-2011*. Washington, D.C.: Center for Applied Research in the Apostolate, Georgetown University, 2011.

Gee, Henry, and William John Hardy, ed., "Act Against Jesuits and Seminarists (1585), 27 Elizabeth, Cap. 2," in *Documents Illustrative of English Church History*, 485-92. New York: Macmillan, 1896. Accessed March 31, 2012. http://history.hanover.edu/texts/engref/er85.htr.:i.

Greeley, Andrew M. *Priests in the United States: Reflections on a Survey*. Garden City, New York: Doubleday & Co., 1972.

Guilday, Peter. *The English Catholic Refugees on the Continent 1558-1795, Vol. 1—The English Colleges and Convents in the Catholic Low Countries*. London: Longmans, Green and Co., 1914. Accessed March 31, 2012. http://books.google.com/books.

Hall, Ryan C. W. and Richard C. W. Hall. "A Profile of Pedophilia: Definition, Characteristics of Offenders, Recidivism, Treatment Outcomes, and Forensic Issues," *Mayo Clinical Proceedings* (2007) 82: 457-71.

Hedin, Raymond. *Married to the Church.* Bloomington, Indiana: Indiana University Press, 1995.

Heisig, James W. "Seminary Education: The Ritualization of Underdevelopment," *Review for Religious* (1975) 34/5: 735–47.

Hendrickson, Paul. *Seminary: A Search.* New York: Summit Books, 1983.

Herbermann, Charles G., Edward A. Pace, Condé B. Pallen, Thomas Shahan and John J. Wynne, eds. *Catholic Encyclopedia*, 15 vols. New York: The Encylopedia Press, 1913. Accessed March 31, 2012. http://books.google.com/books.

Hidalgo, Myra L. *Sexual Abuse and the Culture of Catholicism: How Priests and Nuns Become Perpetrators.* Binghamton, New York: The Haworth Press, 2007.

Hughes, Philip. *A Popular History of the Reformation.* Garden City, New York: Image, 1960.

Jacobs, Henry Ester, ed. *The Works of Martin Luther, with Introductions and Notes.* Philadephia: A. J. Holman Company, 1915. Accessed March 31, 2012. http://books.google.com/books.

John Jay College of Criminal Justice (Terry, Karen et al.). *The Nature and Scope of the Problem of Sexual Abuse of Minors by Priests and Deacons.* Washington D.C.: United States Conference of Catholic Bishops, 2004.

———. *The Causes and Context of Sexual Abuse of Minors by Catholic Priests in the United States, 1950-2010.* Washington D.C.: United States Conference of Catholic Bishops, 2011.

Kelly, Robert J. and Rob Lusk. "Theories of Pedophilia." In *The Sexual Abuse of Children: Theory and Research, Volume 1*, edited by William O'Donohue and James H. Geer. Hillsdale, New Jersey: Lawrence Erlbaum Associates, 1992.

Kenna, Michael. *Boarding School.* Portland, Oregon: Nazraeli Press, 2003.

Kennedy, Eugene C. and Victor J. Heckler. *The Catholic Priest in the United States: Psychological Investigations.* Washington D.C.: United States Catholic Conference, Publications Office, 1972.

Knox, Thomas Francis. *Records of the English Catholics under the Penal Laws...The First and Second Diaries of the English College, Douay.* London: David Nutt, 1878. Accessed March 31, 2012. http://books.google.com/books.

Lone Star College, Kingwood. "American Cultural History: The Twentieth Century." Accessed March 31, 2012. http://wwwappskc.lonestar.edu/popculture/decades.html.

Marshall, Peter. *The Reformation, A Very Short Introduction.* Oxford: OUP Oxford, 2009.

McBrien, Richard P., ed. *The Harper Collins Encyclopedia of Catholicism.* New York: HarperCollins Publishers, 1995.

Miller, Keith. *Wonders of the World: St. Peter's.* Cambridge, Massachusetts: Harvard University Press, 2007.

Möller, Wilhelm Ernst, "Luther's Rupture with Rome." In *History of the Christian Church*, Vol. 3, *Reformation and Counter-Reformation*, edited by G. Kawerau, translated by J. H. Freese. London: Swan Sonnenschein & Co., 1900. Accessed March 31, 2012. http://books.google.com/books.

Murphy, Charles M. *Models of Priestly Formation: Past, Present and Future.* New York: Crossroad Publishing Company, 2006.

National Review Board for the Protection of Children and Young People. *A Report on the Crisis in the Catholic Church in the United States*. Washington: United States Conference of Catholic Bishops, 2004.

Plumb, Brian. "English and Continental Seminaries Conducted by the Secular Clergy," in "The Catholic Historian's Handbook, 1829-1966". Accessed March 31, 2012. http://www.catholic-history.org.uk/nwchs/plumb/seminaries.html.

Osborne, Kenan B., "Priestly Formation." In *From Trent to Vatican 2*, edited by Raymond F. Bulman and Frederick J. Parrella. New York: Oxford University Press, 2006.

Pearsall, Arlene Epp, "Johannes Pauli and the papal indulgence." In *Reform and Counterreform: Dialectics of the Word in Western Christianity Since Luther*, edited by John Charles Hawley. Berlin: Mouton de Gruyter, 1994.

Plante, Thomas. *A Perspective on Clergy Sexual Abuse*. Rev. version, April 2010. Accessed March 31, 2012. http://www.psywww.com/psyrelig/plante.html.

Plante, Thomas G., ed. *Bless Me Father For I Have Sinned: Perspectives on Sexual Abuse Committed by Roman Catholic Priests*. Westport, Connecticut: Praeger Publishers, 1999.

————. *Sin Against the Innocents: Sexual Abuse by Priests and the Role of the Catholic Church*. Westport, Connecticut: Praeger Publishers, 2004.

Podles, Leon J. *Sacrilege: Sexual Abuse in the Catholic Church*. Baltimore: Crossland Press, 2008.

Prentky, Robert A., Raymond A. Knight, and Austin F.S. Lee. *Child Sexual Molestation: Research Issues*. National Institute of Justice, Washington D.C., 1997.

Public Broadcasting Service. *American Experience: The Pill*. Accessed March 31, 2012. http://www.pbs.org/wgbh/amex/pill/index.html.

Rose, Michael S. *Goodbye, Good Men: How Liberals Brought Corruption into the Catholic Church*. Washington: Regnery Publishing, 2002.

Rowan, Edward L. *Understanding Child Sexual Abuse*. Jackson, Mississippi: University Press of Mississippi, 2006.

Sipe, A. W. Richard. *A Secret World: Sexuality and the Search for Celibacy*. New York: Brunner/Mazel, 1990.

————. *Celibacy in Crisis: A Secret World Revisited*. New York: Brunner-Routledge, 2003.

Smith, S. B. "Duties of Bishops in regard to the Management of Ecclesiastical Seminaries —Of Seminaries in the United States," *Elements of Ecclesiastical Law*, 343-348. New York: Benziger Brothers, 1893. Accessed March 31, 2012. http://books.google.com/books.

Snead-Cox, John George. "The Education of the Priest," in *The Life of Cardinal Vaughn*, Vol. 2. London: Herbert and Daniel, 1910. Accessed March 31, 2012. http://books.google.com/books.

Sperry, Len. *Sex, Priestly Ministry and the Church*. Collegeville, Minnesota: Liturgical Press, 2003.

St. Mary's Seminary of St. Sulpice. *Memorial Volume of the Centenary of St. Mary's Seminary of St. Sulpice*. Baltimore: John Murphy & Co.,1891. Accessed March 31, 2012. http://books.google.com/books.

Pope Pius XII. Menti Nostrae, *Apostolic Exhortation to the Clergy of the Entire World on the Development of Holiness in Priestly Life*, 1950. Accessed March 31, 2012. http://www.ewtn.com/library/papaldoc/p12clerg.htm.

Pope Paul VI. *Decree on Priestly Training* Optatam Totius *Proclaimed By His Holiness Pope Paul VI On October 28, 1965*. Accessed March 31, 2012.

http://www.vatican.va/archive/hist_councils/ii_vatican_council/documents/
    vat-ii_decree_19651028_optatam-totius_en.html.
United States Conference of Catholic Bishops, "Child and Youth Protection." Accessed
    May 18, 2012. http://www.usccb.org/issues-and-action/child-and-youth-protection/.
Vatican, The Holy See. "Abuse of Minors. The Church Response." Accessed May 18,
    2012. http://www.vatican.va/resources/index_en.htm.
Waterworth, J. (transl.). *The Canons and Decrees of the Sacred and Oecumenical
    Council of Trent*. London: Dolman, 1848. Accessed March 31, 2012.
    http://history.hanover.edu/texts/trent/ct23.html.
Wikipedia. "Roman Catholic sex abuse cases by country." Accessed May 18, 2012.
    http://en.wikipedia.org/wiki/Roman_Catholic_sex_abuse_cases_by_country.
———.   "Ushaw   College."   Accessed   March   31,   2012.
    http://en.wikipedia.org/wiki/Ushaw_College.